Ace Academic Publishing
ACHIEVING EXCELLENCE TOGETHER

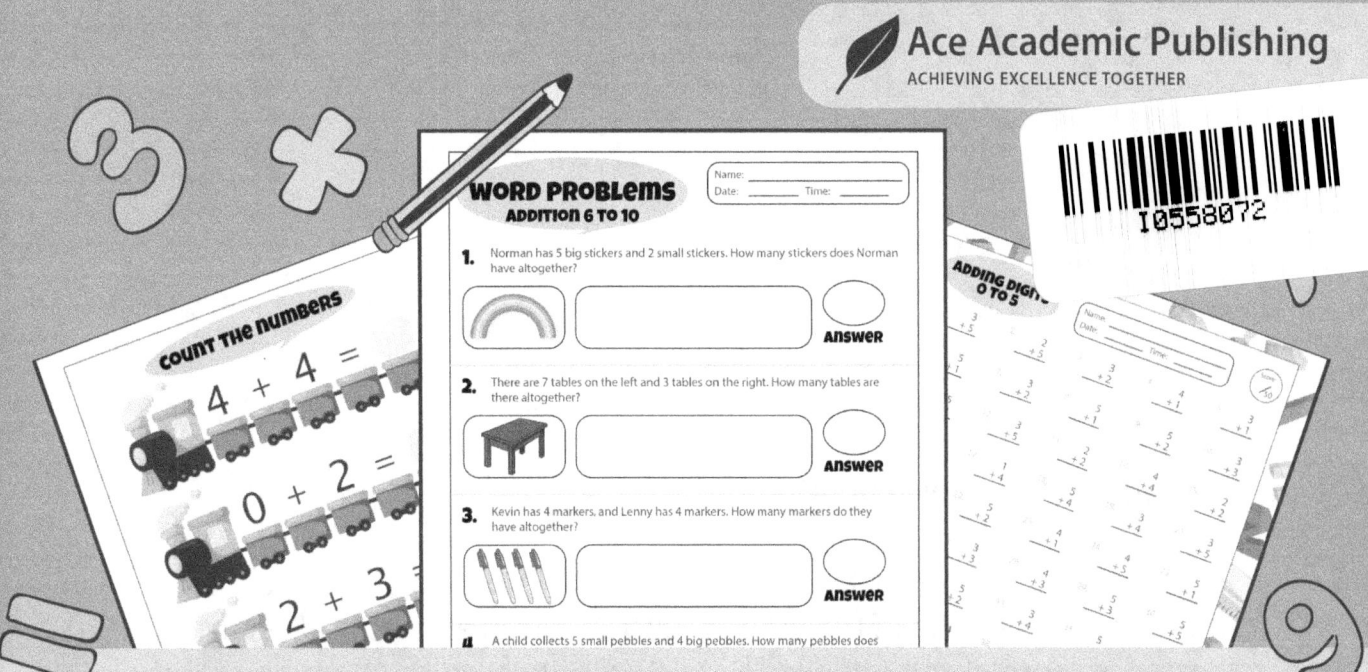

SIMPLE MATH!

200 WORD PROBLEMS WITH ANSWERS | **3000+FACT WORKSHEETS**

ADDITION AND SUBTRACTION

SEVERAL FUN ACTIVITIES

www.aceacademicpublishing.com

Author: Ace Academic Publishing

Prepaze is a sister company of Ace Academic Publishing. Intrigued by the unending possibilities of the internet and its role in education, Prepaze was created to spread the knowledge and learning across all corners of the world through an online platform. We equip ourselves with state-of-the-art technologies so that knowledge reaches the students through the quickest and the most effective channels.

The materials for our books are written by award winning teachers with several years of teaching experience. All our books are aligned with the state standards and are widely used by many schools throughout the country.

For enquiries and bulk order, contact us at the following address:

3031 Village Market Place,
Morrisville, NC 27560
www.aceacademicpublishing.com

Ace Academic Publishing
ACHIEVING EXCELLENCE TOGETHER

ISBN: 978-1-962517-18-8

PARENT'S GUIDE

This book is suitable for kids in the age range of 4-8. The book contains several pages of math fact tests that can be an excellent practice to increase fluency in basic math operations. Not only that, but the book also contains 200-word problems that can also help your student apply the facts that they have practiced. We always try to ensure that the kids have a fun learning experience and so we have also included several fun activities. This is an excellent book for your kids to practice facts, understand word problems, and have fun with them!

Ace Academic Publishing
ACHIEVING EXCELLENCE TOGETHER

Other books from Ace Academic Publishing

Ace Academic Publishing

ACHIEVING EXCELLENCE TOGETHER

TABLE OF CONTENTS

HELLO EVERYONE!

Let's learn
math with

ADDITION

Shall we start?
Let's go!

ADDITION

The process of combining two or more quantities is called addition. The addition is one of the four basic operations of arithmetic. When the numbers are added together, the result is called the sum or total. The symbol used to represent addition is '+', commonly known as a plus.

Example:

$4 + 1 = 5$

To add 4 and 1, we can count forward 1 step from 4.

Which can be represented in number line as follows,

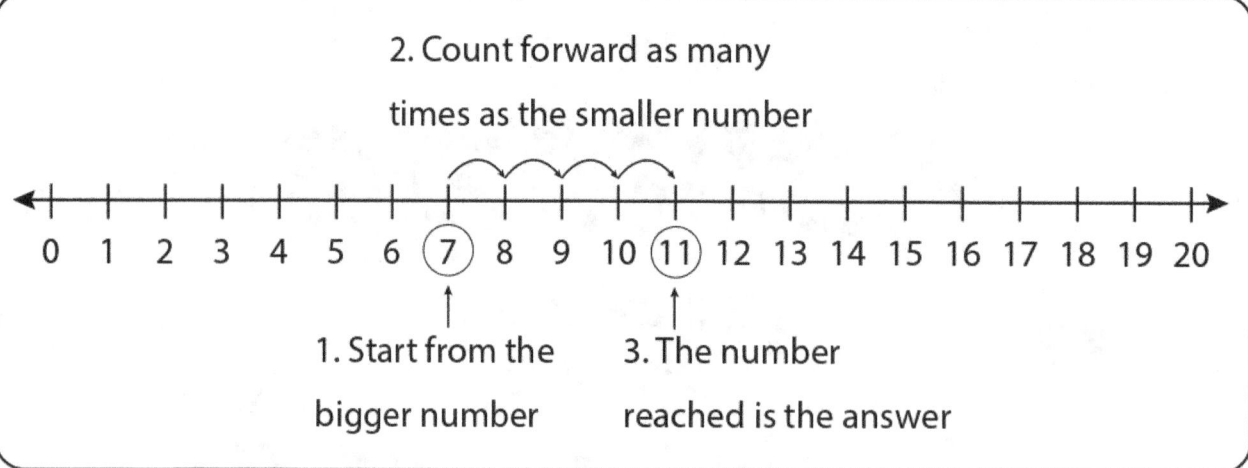

An addition sentence is a mathematical expression that shows the quantities added together and their sum.

We can write the mathematical expression for 7 plus 8 equals 15 as:

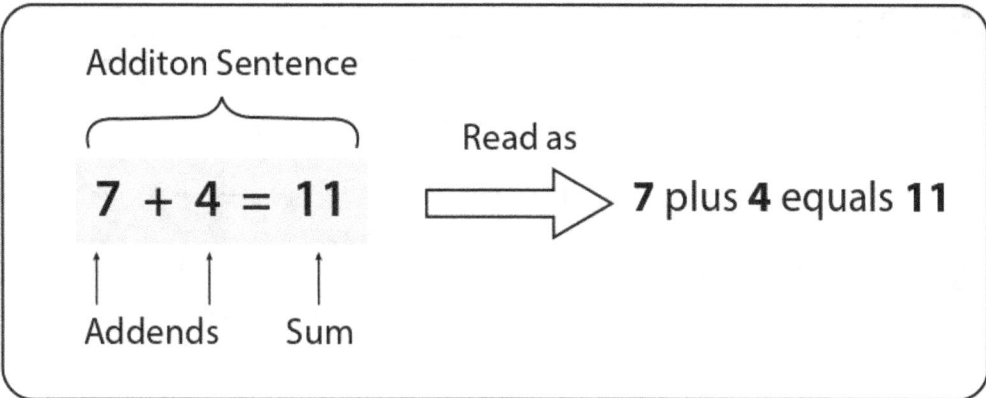

Additon Sentence

7 + 4 = 11

Addends   Sum

Read as ⟹ **7** plus **4** equals **11**

The numbers that are added are called addends and the result to addition is called the sum or total. In an addition sentence, the addends are added to get the sum.

There are different ways to add quantities:

➤ Addition of small numbers can be done using your fingers.

➤ Number charts can be used.

➤ Number line is another way to add small numbers.

➤ Numbers can also be added vertically and horizontally too.

prepaze

1. $\begin{array}{r} 3 \\ +5 \\ \hline \end{array}$	2. $\begin{array}{r} 2 \\ +5 \\ \hline \end{array}$	3. $\begin{array}{r} 3 \\ +2 \\ \hline \end{array}$	4. $\begin{array}{r} 4 \\ +1 \\ \hline \end{array}$	5. $\begin{array}{r} 3 \\ +1 \\ \hline \end{array}$
6. $\begin{array}{r} 5 \\ +1 \\ \hline \end{array}$	7. $\begin{array}{r} 3 \\ +2 \\ \hline \end{array}$	8. $\begin{array}{r} 5 \\ +1 \\ \hline \end{array}$	9. $\begin{array}{r} 5 \\ +2 \\ \hline \end{array}$	10. $\begin{array}{r} 3 \\ +3 \\ \hline \end{array}$
11. $\begin{array}{r} 5 \\ +2 \\ \hline \end{array}$	12. $\begin{array}{r} 3 \\ +5 \\ \hline \end{array}$	13. $\begin{array}{r} 2 \\ +2 \\ \hline \end{array}$	14. $\begin{array}{r} 4 \\ +4 \\ \hline \end{array}$	15. $\begin{array}{r} 2 \\ +2 \\ \hline \end{array}$
16. $\begin{array}{r} 1 \\ +5 \\ \hline \end{array}$	17. $\begin{array}{r} 1 \\ +4 \\ \hline \end{array}$	18. $\begin{array}{r} 5 \\ +4 \\ \hline \end{array}$	19. $\begin{array}{r} 3 \\ +4 \\ \hline \end{array}$	20. $\begin{array}{r} 3 \\ +5 \\ \hline \end{array}$
21. $\begin{array}{r} 1 \\ +3 \\ \hline \end{array}$	22. $\begin{array}{r} 5 \\ +2 \\ \hline \end{array}$	23. $\begin{array}{r} 4 \\ +1 \\ \hline \end{array}$	24. $\begin{array}{r} 4 \\ +5 \\ \hline \end{array}$	25. $\begin{array}{r} 5 \\ +1 \\ \hline \end{array}$
26. $\begin{array}{r} 1 \\ +4 \\ \hline \end{array}$	27. $\begin{array}{r} 3 \\ +3 \\ \hline \end{array}$	28. $\begin{array}{r} 4 \\ +3 \\ \hline \end{array}$	29. $\begin{array}{r} 5 \\ +3 \\ \hline \end{array}$	30. $\begin{array}{r} 5 \\ +5 \\ \hline \end{array}$
31. $\begin{array}{r} 4 \\ +1 \\ \hline \end{array}$	32. $\begin{array}{r} 5 \\ +2 \\ \hline \end{array}$	33. $\begin{array}{r} 3 \\ +4 \\ \hline \end{array}$	34. $\begin{array}{r} 5 \\ +1 \\ \hline \end{array}$	35. $\begin{array}{r} 4 \\ +3 \\ \hline \end{array}$
36. $\begin{array}{r} 4 \\ +5 \\ \hline \end{array}$	37. $\begin{array}{r} 4 \\ +4 \\ \hline \end{array}$	38. $\begin{array}{r} 2 \\ +4 \\ \hline \end{array}$	39. $\begin{array}{r} 2 \\ +2 \\ \hline \end{array}$	40. $\begin{array}{r} 1 \\ +1 \\ \hline \end{array}$
41. $\begin{array}{r} 2 \\ +3 \\ \hline \end{array}$	42. $\begin{array}{r} 5 \\ +2 \\ \hline \end{array}$	43. $\begin{array}{r} 1 \\ +5 \\ \hline \end{array}$	44. $\begin{array}{r} 1 \\ +3 \\ \hline \end{array}$	45. $\begin{array}{r} 2 \\ +1 \\ \hline \end{array}$
46. $\begin{array}{r} 3 \\ +1 \\ \hline \end{array}$	47. $\begin{array}{r} 5 \\ +2 \\ \hline \end{array}$	48. $\begin{array}{r} 5 \\ +3 \\ \hline \end{array}$	49. $\begin{array}{r} 2 \\ +4 \\ \hline \end{array}$	50. $\begin{array}{r} 1 \\ +5 \\ \hline \end{array}$

ADDITION 0 TO 5

1. $\begin{array}{r} 4 \\ +4 \\ \hline \end{array}$	2. $\begin{array}{r} 5 \\ +1 \\ \hline \end{array}$	3. $\begin{array}{r} 1 \\ +2 \\ \hline \end{array}$	4. $\begin{array}{r} 5 \\ +4 \\ \hline \end{array}$	5. $\begin{array}{r} 5 \\ +5 \\ \hline \end{array}$
6. $\begin{array}{r} 1 \\ +5 \\ \hline \end{array}$	7. $\begin{array}{r} 2 \\ +2 \\ \hline \end{array}$	8. $\begin{array}{r} 4 \\ +2 \\ \hline \end{array}$	9. $\begin{array}{r} 3 \\ +2 \\ \hline \end{array}$	10. $\begin{array}{r} 4 \\ +4 \\ \hline \end{array}$
11. $\begin{array}{r} 5 \\ +2 \\ \hline \end{array}$	12. $\begin{array}{r} 3 \\ +2 \\ \hline \end{array}$	13. $\begin{array}{r} 2 \\ +4 \\ \hline \end{array}$	14. $\begin{array}{r} 5 \\ +4 \\ \hline \end{array}$	15. $\begin{array}{r} 1 \\ +4 \\ \hline \end{array}$
16. $\begin{array}{r} 3 \\ +4 \\ \hline \end{array}$	17. $\begin{array}{r} 1 \\ +3 \\ \hline \end{array}$	18. $\begin{array}{r} 1 \\ +1 \\ \hline \end{array}$	19. $\begin{array}{r} 5 \\ +3 \\ \hline \end{array}$	20. $\begin{array}{r} 5 \\ +2 \\ \hline \end{array}$
21. $\begin{array}{r} 1 \\ +1 \\ \hline \end{array}$	22. $\begin{array}{r} 2 \\ +2 \\ \hline \end{array}$	23. $\begin{array}{r} 2 \\ +5 \\ \hline \end{array}$	24. $\begin{array}{r} 1 \\ +3 \\ \hline \end{array}$	25. $\begin{array}{r} 5 \\ +4 \\ \hline \end{array}$
26. $\begin{array}{r} 4 \\ +5 \\ \hline \end{array}$	27. $\begin{array}{r} 5 \\ +3 \\ \hline \end{array}$	28. $\begin{array}{r} 5 \\ +5 \\ \hline \end{array}$	29. $\begin{array}{r} 1 \\ +3 \\ \hline \end{array}$	30. $\begin{array}{r} 2 \\ +5 \\ \hline \end{array}$
31. $\begin{array}{r} 4 \\ +2 \\ \hline \end{array}$	32. $\begin{array}{r} 4 \\ +3 \\ \hline \end{array}$	33. $\begin{array}{r} 4 \\ +1 \\ \hline \end{array}$	34. $\begin{array}{r} 2 \\ +2 \\ \hline \end{array}$	35. $\begin{array}{r} 5 \\ +5 \\ \hline \end{array}$
36. $\begin{array}{r} 4 \\ +3 \\ \hline \end{array}$	37. $\begin{array}{r} 4 \\ +2 \\ \hline \end{array}$	38. $\begin{array}{r} 3 \\ +5 \\ \hline \end{array}$	39. $\begin{array}{r} 5 \\ +2 \\ \hline \end{array}$	40. $\begin{array}{r} 1 \\ +3 \\ \hline \end{array}$
41. $\begin{array}{r} 3 \\ +2 \\ \hline \end{array}$	42. $\begin{array}{r} 1 \\ +1 \\ \hline \end{array}$	43. $\begin{array}{r} 3 \\ +1 \\ \hline \end{array}$	44. $\begin{array}{r} 5 \\ +2 \\ \hline \end{array}$	45. $\begin{array}{r} 2 \\ +1 \\ \hline \end{array}$
46. $\begin{array}{r} 1 \\ +3 \\ \hline \end{array}$	47. $\begin{array}{r} 2 \\ +1 \\ \hline \end{array}$	48. $\begin{array}{r} 5 \\ +4 \\ \hline \end{array}$	49. $\begin{array}{r} 2 \\ +3 \\ \hline \end{array}$	50. $\begin{array}{r} 4 \\ +1 \\ \hline \end{array}$

ADDITION 0 TO 5

1. 5 + 3

2. 1 + 5

3. 2 + 2

4. 4 + 5

5. 2 + 2

6. 1 + 5

7. 3 + 2

8. 2 + 1

9. 4 + 5

10. 4 + 4

11. 1 + 2

12. 3 + 2

13. 4 + 2

14. 5 + 3

15. 3 + 2

16. 2 + 2

17. 2 + 4

18. 5 + 2

19. 2 + 3

20. 1 + 2

21. 1 + 4

22. 1 + 3

23. 4 + 4

24. 3 + 2

25. 5 + 4

26. 4 + 1

27. 3 + 5

28. 5 + 4

29. 4 + 4

30. 4 + 5

31. 3 + 1

32. 3 + 5

33. 1 + 4

34. 3 + 3

35. 1 + 5

36. 4 + 4

37. 1 + 4

38. 1 + 1

39. 2 + 2

40. 4 + 5

41. 3 + 1

42. 5 + 4

43. 4 + 1

44. 1 + 2

45. 3 + 3

46. 5 + 4

47. 5 + 5

48. 1 + 4

49. 5 + 3

50. 5 + 2

1. 2 +5	2. 4 +3	3. 4 +5	4. 1 +3	5. 3 +4
6. 4 +1	7. 2 +2	8. 5 +5	9. 5 +3	10. 2 +1
11. 2 +4	12. 1 +5	13. 4 +2	14. 3 +3	15. 2 +3
16. 5 +4	17. 2 +3	18. 4 +3	19. 1 +2	20. 5 +4
21. 1 +2	22. 2 +5	23. 2 +4	24. 4 +4	25. 3 +4
26. 4 +4	27. 3 +1	28. 3 +5	29. 5 +5	30. 5 +3
31. 2 +1	32. 3 +5	33. 5 +1	34. 5 +4	35. 4 +1
36. 3 +3	37. 3 +5	38. 4 +5	39. 3 +1	40. 3 +5
41. 2 +3	42. 5 +2	43. 1 +5	44. 1 +3	45. 2 +1
46. 1 +3	47. 5 +4	48. 4 +1	49. 1 +1	50. 2 +4

ADDITION 0 TO 5

1. 4
   + 4
   ____

2. 2
   + 1
   ____

3. 3
   + 5
   ____

4. 4
   + 4
   ____

5. 2
   + 2
   ____

6. 5
   + 4
   ____

7. 1
   + 4
   ____

8. 3
   + 5
   ____

9. 3
   + 4
   ____

10. 4
    + 2
    ____

11. 5
    + 3
    ____

12. 3
    + 1
    ____

13. 5
    + 2
    ____

14. 4
    + 5
    ____

15. 3
    + 2
    ____

16. 3
    + 4
    ____

17. 1
    + 2
    ____

18. 2
    + 5
    ____

19. 5
    + 1
    ____

20. 3
    + 1
    ____

21. 2
    + 3
    ____

22. 4
    + 2
    ____

23. 1
    + 3
    ____

24. 4
    + 1
    ____

25. 5
    + 4
    ____

26. 4
    + 5
    ____

27. 3
    + 4
    ____

28. 2
    + 5
    ____

29. 5
    + 3
    ____

30. 2
    + 5
    ____

31. 4
    + 5
    ____

32. 2
    + 4
    ____

33. 3
    + 4
    ____

34. 3
    + 1
    ____

35. 3
    + 5
    ____

36. 4
    + 3
    ____

37. 2
    + 1
    ____

38. 3
    + 5
    ____

39. 2
    + 5
    ____

40. 3
    + 2
    ____

41. 1
    + 3
    ____

42. 1
    + 5
    ____

43. 1
    + 2
    ____

44. 5
    + 5
    ____

45. 3
    + 5
    ____

46. 3
    + 1
    ____

47. 5
    + 1
    ____

48. 4
    + 5
    ____

49. 1
    + 2
    ____

50. 3
    + 3
    ____

1. 4
    + 1

2. 1
    + 1

3. 5
    + 3

4. 2
    + 1

5. 2
    + 3

6. 5
    + 5

7. 3
    + 2

8. 3
    + 1

9. 5
    + 5

10. 2
    + 3

11. 4
    + 1

12. 2
    + 3

13. 1
    + 1

14. 3
    + 5

15. 2
    + 1

16. 4
    + 4

17. 1
    + 3

18. 4
    + 1

19. 5
    + 4

20. 1
    + 1

21. 1
    + 5

22. 4
    + 4

23. 1
    + 1

24. 5
    + 5

25. 2
    + 2

26. 1
    + 4

27. 3
    + 3

28. 4
    + 3

29. 5
    + 3

30. 5
    + 5

31. 3
    + 3

32. 3
    + 4

33. 1
    + 3

34. 3
    + 2

35. 1
    + 2

36. 5
    + 2

37. 5
    + 5

38. 3
    + 4

39. 2
    + 1

40. 5
    + 5

41. 1
    + 3

42. 5
    + 3

43. 4
    + 4

44. 2
    + 5

45. 2
    + 2

46. 3
    + 2

47. 5
    + 1

48. 5
    + 5

49. 3
    + 3

50. 4
    + 1

ADDITION 0 TO 5

1. 2 + 2
2. 4 + 1
3. 4 + 2
4. 4 + 4
5. 3 + 1

6. 1 + 2
7. 4 + 3
8. 5 + 1
9. 1 + 3
10. 4 + 4

11. 4 + 5
12. 2 + 3
13. 4 + 4
14. 4 + 5
15. 2 + 2

16. 4 + 2
17. 1 + 4
18. 5 + 1
19. 4 + 2
20. 2 + 3

21. 5 + 1
22. 3 + 5
23. 2 + 1
24. 4 + 3
25. 4 + 1

26. 2 + 5
27. 2 + 4
28. 2 + 2
29. 3 + 1
30. 1 + 4

31. 5 + 2
32. 1 + 5
33. 1 + 3
34. 1 + 1
35. 3 + 3

36. 1 + 5
37. 4 + 5
38. 4 + 5
39. 2 + 4
40. 3 + 4

41. 5 + 5
42. 4 + 2
43. 1 + 1
44. 2 + 2
45. 4 + 2

46. 4 + 1
47. 3 + 3
48. 3 + 1
49. 1 + 5
50. 1 + 2

Name: _____

Date: _____ Time: _____

Score: /50

1. 4 +2	2. 5 +5	3. 4 +5	4. 4 +2	5. 2 +3
6. 5 +4	7. 3 +4	8. 2 +5	9. 1 +5	10. 5 +2
11. 1 +2	12. 5 +1	13. 5 +4	14. 4 +2	15. 4 +4
16. 3 +5	17. 5 +2	18. 5 +1	19. 4 +4	20. 1 +3
21. 2 +5	22. 3 +2	23. 3 +5	24. 2 +3	25. 2 +5
26. 4 +2	27. 5 +2	28. 2 +2	29. 4 +3	30. 5 +4
31. 5 +3	32. 1 +2	33. 5 +4	34. 4 +4	35. 5 +2
36. 1 +5	37. 4 +2	38. 2 +2	39. 4 +3	40. 2 +4
41. 1 +4	42. 5 +5	43. 4 +3	44. 5 +5	45. 2 +3
46. 2 +5	47. 3 +4	48. 1 +2	49. 4 +2	50. 2 +2

prepaze

ADD THE NUMBERS

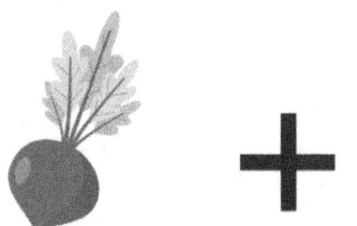 **+**  **=**

 **+**  **=**

 **+**   **=**

 **+**  **=**

Name: _____

Date: _____ Time: _____

1. Jared and Hanna have 2 cupcakes. Then they make 1 more cupcake. How many cupcakes do they have now?

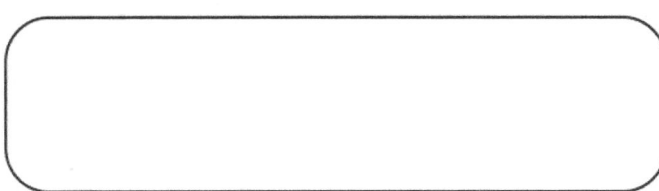

ANSWER

2. Rose has 2 coloring books. Her father buys her 2 more coloring books. How many coloring books does Rose have now?

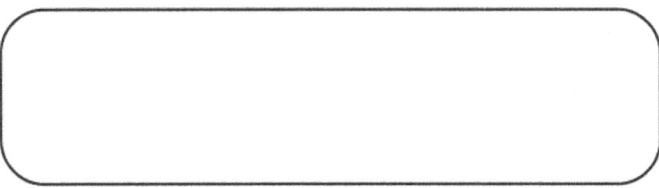

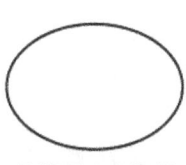

ANSWER

3. Anna used the laptop for 1 hour. Her brother used the laptop for 1 hour. How many hours did they use the laptop altogether?

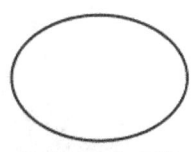

ANSWER

4. John has 1 pencil. His friend gives him 2 pencils. How many pencils does John have?

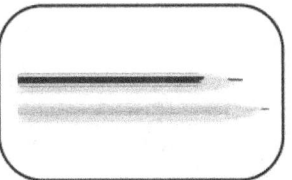

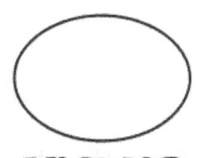

ANSWER

5. Luke practices piano 1 hour in the morning and 1 hour in the evening. How many hours does he practice piano in a day?

ANSWER

6. Tom has a candy. His sister gives him 2 more candies. How many candies does he have now?

 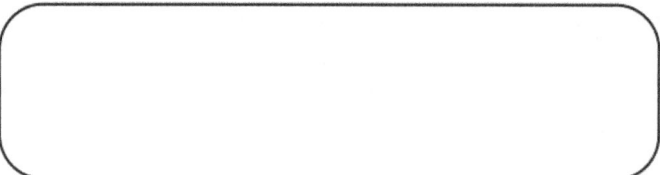 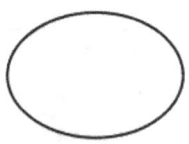

ANSWER

7. Alex arranges 3 books on her study table. She places one more book on the table. How many books are there now?

 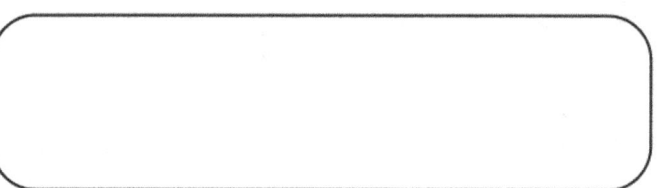 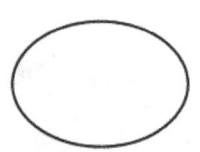

ANSWER

8. Aaron has 3 carrots. He buys 2 more carrots. How many carrots does he have now?

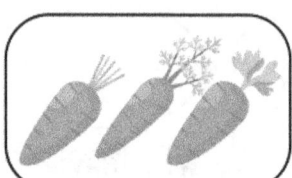 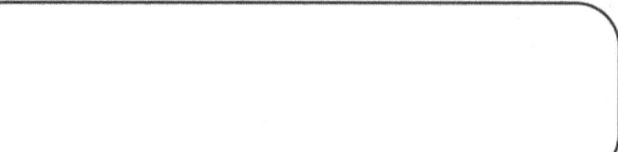 

ANSWER

WORD PROBLEMS
ADDITION 0 TO 5

9. Joey has 2 pairs of white socks and 2 pairs of black socks. How many pairs of socks does she have

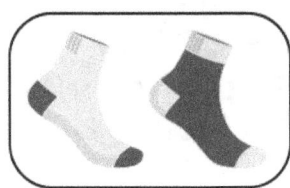

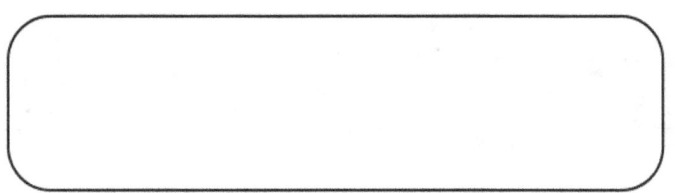

ANSWER

10. Eliot knows 2 songs. He learned 3 more songs. How many songs does Eliot know?

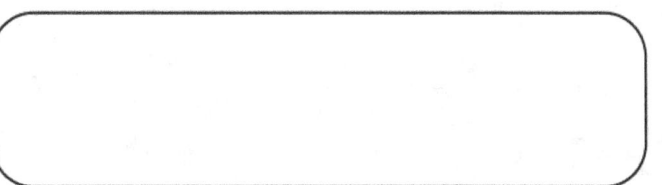

ANSWER

11. There are 4 children in the park. One more child joins them. How many children are in the park now?

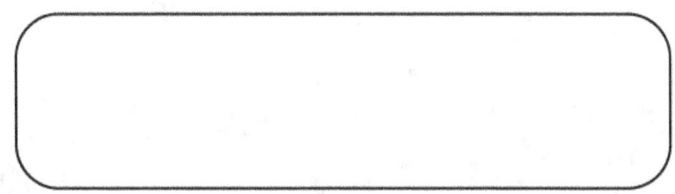

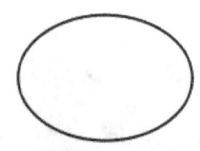

ANSWER

12. There are 3 candles on a cake. Mom adds 1 more candle. How many candles are there now?

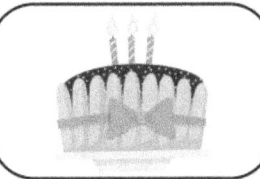

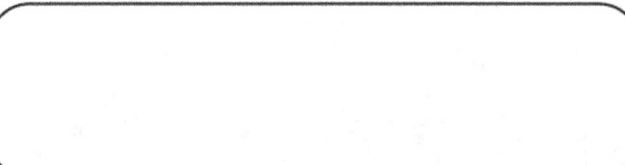

ANSWER

ADD THE NUMBERS

4 + 4 =

0 + 2 =

2 + 3 =

5 + 1 =

WORD PROBLEMS
ADDITION 0 TO 5

Name: _____

Date: _____ Time: _____

13. Pam has $1 and Mark has $1. How much money do they have in all?

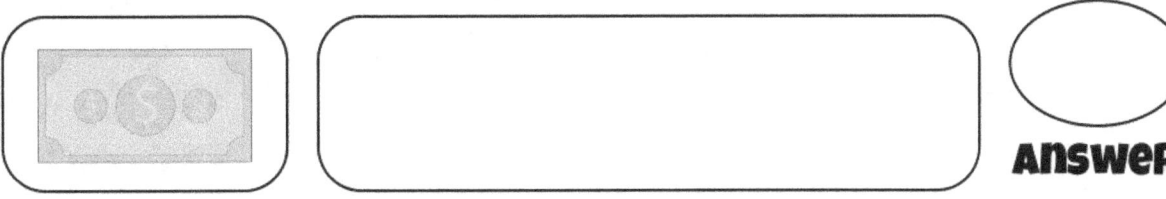

answer

14. Casey has 2 toys and her friend has 1 toy. How many toys do they have together?

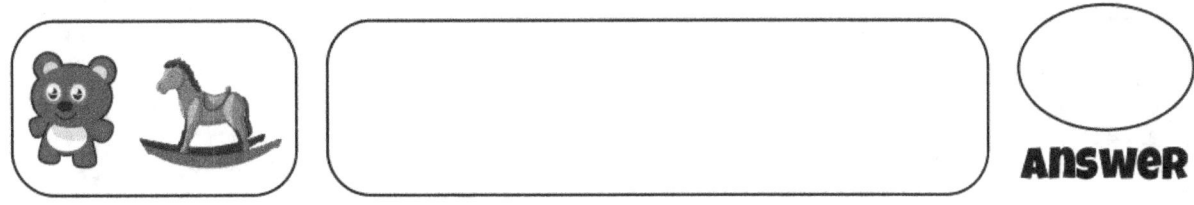

answer

15. Erick has 3 marbles and Vega has 2 marbles. How many marbles do they have in all?

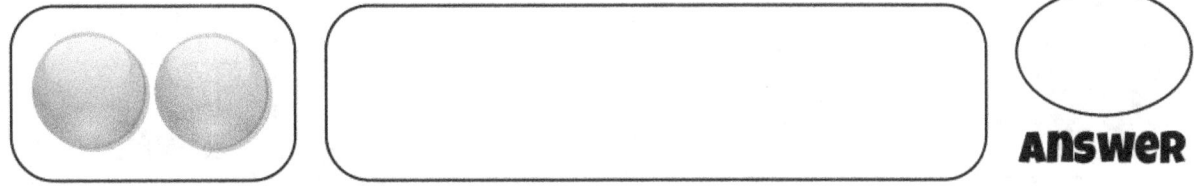

answer

16. Amy ate two strawberries. Then she ate two more strawberries. How may strawberries did she eat?

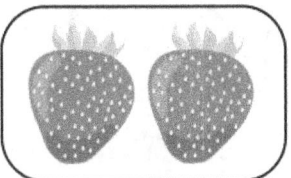

answer

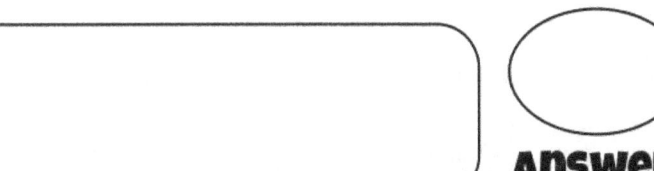

Name: _____

Date: _____ Time: _____

17. Toni had a pet hamster. His brother gave him hamster for his birthday. How many hamsters does Toni have now?

 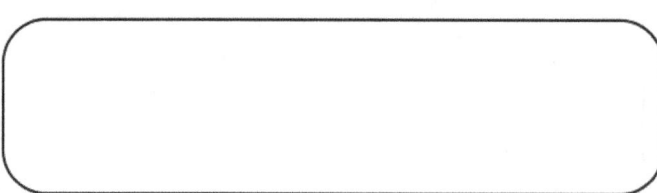 

ANSWER

18. Tammy lost an eraser last week. She lost 2 erasers this week. How many erasers did she lose in two weeks?

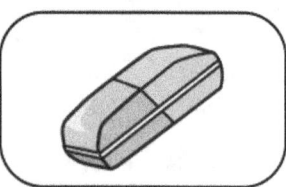 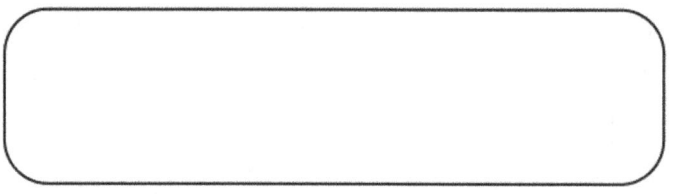

ANSWER

19. Joshua saw a butterfly on his window. He then saw 3 butterflies in the garden. How many butterflies did he see in all?

 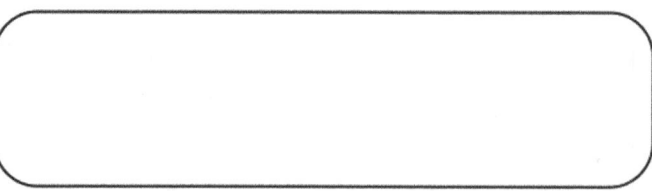 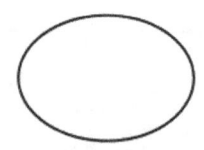

ANSWER

20. There are 4 birds on a tree. One more bird joins them. How many birds are there on the tree now?

ANSWER

WORD PROBLEMS
ADDITION 0 TO 5

Name: _____
Date: _____ Time: _____

21. Ray has 2 big balls and 3 small balls. How many balls does he have?

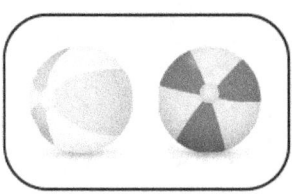

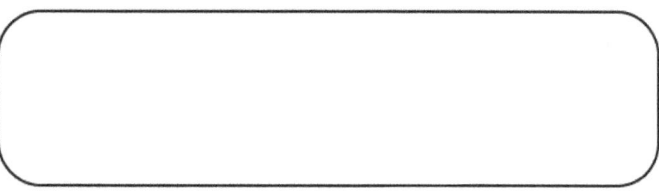

ANSWER

22. We have a cookie jar. We buy one more cookie jar. How many cookie jars do we have now?

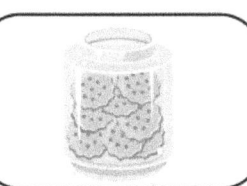

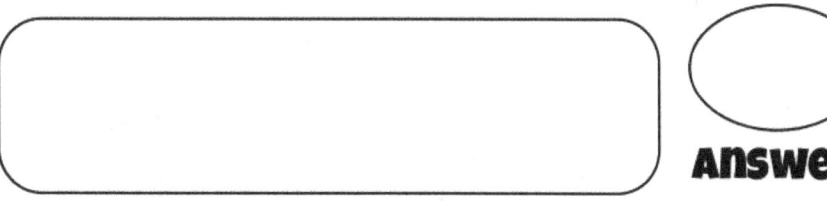

ANSWER

23. There are 2 people in the car. 2 more people join them on the way. How many people are there in the car?

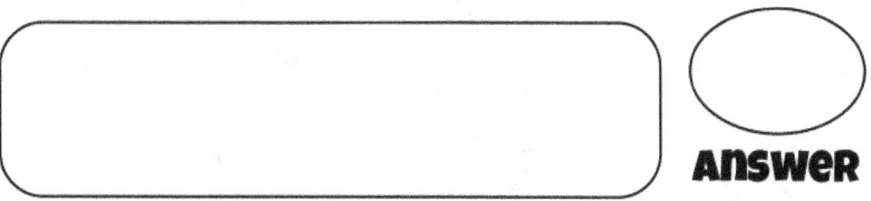

ANSWER

24. Nick has two baskets. His sister gives him 1 more basket. How many baskets does he have now?

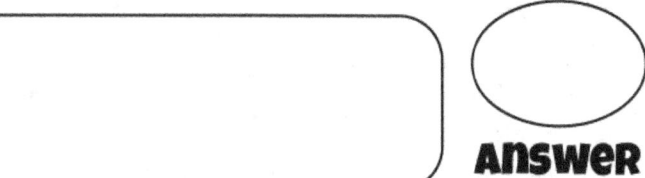

ANSWER

prepaze

WORD PROBLEMS
ADDITION 0 TO 5

Name: ____________________

Date: __________ Time: __________

25. Katie paints 1 chair. Then she paints 4 more chairs. How many chairs does she paint in all?

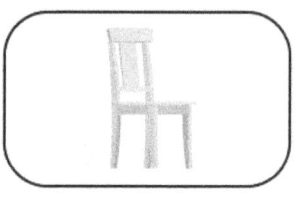

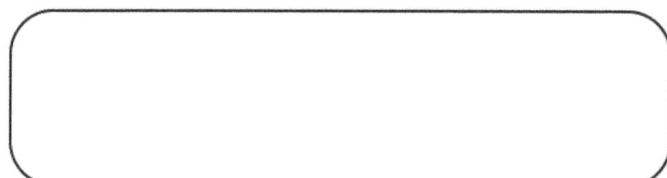

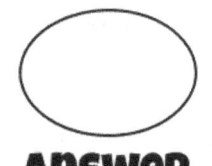

ANSWER

ACTIVITY CORNER

FIND A WAY

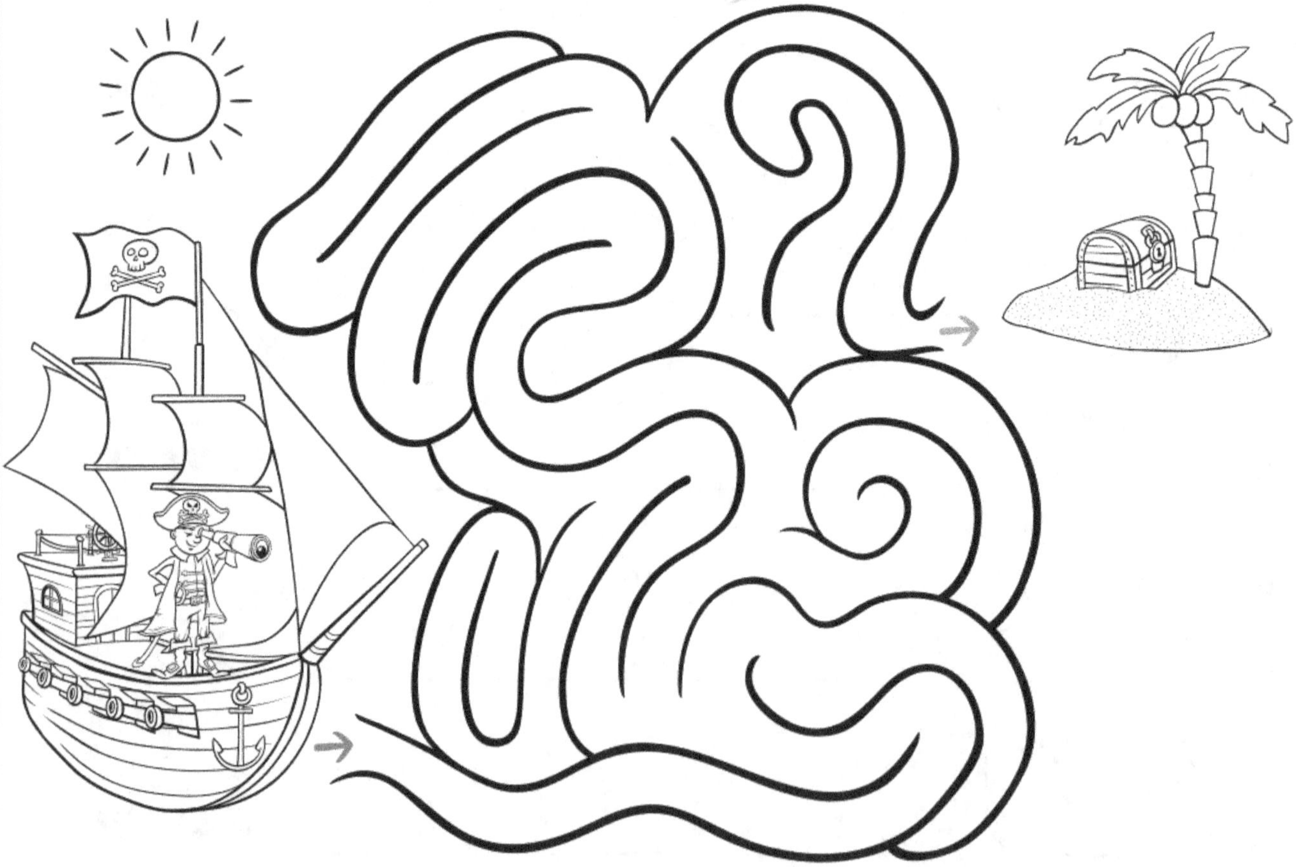

ADDITION 6 TO 10

Name: _____

Date: _____ Time: _____

Score: __/50

1. $\begin{array}{r} 8 \\ +10 \\ \hline \end{array}$	2. $\begin{array}{r} 9 \\ +8 \\ \hline \end{array}$	3. $\begin{array}{r} 9 \\ +9 \\ \hline \end{array}$	4. $\begin{array}{r} 9 \\ +8 \\ \hline \end{array}$	5. $\begin{array}{r} 9 \\ +6 \\ \hline \end{array}$
6. $\begin{array}{r} 7 \\ +9 \\ \hline \end{array}$	7. $\begin{array}{r} 10 \\ +9 \\ \hline \end{array}$	8. $\begin{array}{r} 9 \\ +6 \\ \hline \end{array}$	9. $\begin{array}{r} 6 \\ +6 \\ \hline \end{array}$	10. $\begin{array}{r} 7 \\ +8 \\ \hline \end{array}$
11. $\begin{array}{r} 8 \\ +8 \\ \hline \end{array}$	12. $\begin{array}{r} 9 \\ +9 \\ \hline \end{array}$	13. $\begin{array}{r} 9 \\ +9 \\ \hline \end{array}$	14. $\begin{array}{r} 7 \\ +7 \\ \hline \end{array}$	15. $\begin{array}{r} 7 \\ +6 \\ \hline \end{array}$
16. $\begin{array}{r} 7 \\ +8 \\ \hline \end{array}$	17. $\begin{array}{r} 7 \\ +9 \\ \hline \end{array}$	18. $\begin{array}{r} 6 \\ +8 \\ \hline \end{array}$	19. $\begin{array}{r} 7 \\ +9 \\ \hline \end{array}$	20. $\begin{array}{r} 7 \\ +8 \\ \hline \end{array}$
21. $\begin{array}{r} 8 \\ +9 \\ \hline \end{array}$	22. $\begin{array}{r} 10 \\ +9 \\ \hline \end{array}$	23. $\begin{array}{r} 9 \\ +10 \\ \hline \end{array}$	24. $\begin{array}{r} 8 \\ +10 \\ \hline \end{array}$	25. $\begin{array}{r} 7 \\ +8 \\ \hline \end{array}$
26. $\begin{array}{r} 7 \\ +6 \\ \hline \end{array}$	27. $\begin{array}{r} 9 \\ +6 \\ \hline \end{array}$	28. $\begin{array}{r} 7 \\ +9 \\ \hline \end{array}$	29. $\begin{array}{r} 6 \\ +7 \\ \hline \end{array}$	30. $\begin{array}{r} 7 \\ +8 \\ \hline \end{array}$
31. $\begin{array}{r} 8 \\ +9 \\ \hline \end{array}$	32. $\begin{array}{r} 10 \\ +9 \\ \hline \end{array}$	33. $\begin{array}{r} 10 \\ +9 \\ \hline \end{array}$	34. $\begin{array}{r} 7 \\ +9 \\ \hline \end{array}$	35. $\begin{array}{r} 7 \\ +9 \\ \hline \end{array}$
36. $\begin{array}{r} 9 \\ +9 \\ \hline \end{array}$	37. $\begin{array}{r} 7 \\ +10 \\ \hline \end{array}$	38. $\begin{array}{r} 6 \\ +9 \\ \hline \end{array}$	39. $\begin{array}{r} 9 \\ +10 \\ \hline \end{array}$	40. $\begin{array}{r} 7 \\ +8 \\ \hline \end{array}$
41. $\begin{array}{r} 10 \\ +9 \\ \hline \end{array}$	42. $\begin{array}{r} 6 \\ +8 \\ \hline \end{array}$	43. $\begin{array}{r} 8 \\ +9 \\ \hline \end{array}$	44. $\begin{array}{r} 7 \\ +9 \\ \hline \end{array}$	45. $\begin{array}{r} 9 \\ +9 \\ \hline \end{array}$
46. $\begin{array}{r} 7 \\ +8 \\ \hline \end{array}$	47. $\begin{array}{r} 10 \\ +9 \\ \hline \end{array}$	48. $\begin{array}{r} 9 \\ +8 \\ \hline \end{array}$	49. $\begin{array}{r} 7 \\ +9 \\ \hline \end{array}$	50. $\begin{array}{r} 8 \\ +7 \\ \hline \end{array}$

prepaze

1. $\begin{array}{r} 6 \\ +10 \\ \hline \end{array}$	2. $\begin{array}{r} 9 \\ +7 \\ \hline \end{array}$	3. $\begin{array}{r} 8 \\ +6 \\ \hline \end{array}$	4. $\begin{array}{r} 9 \\ +10 \\ \hline \end{array}$	5. $\begin{array}{r} 7 \\ +8 \\ \hline \end{array}$
6. $\begin{array}{r} 8 \\ +10 \\ \hline \end{array}$	7. $\begin{array}{r} 9 \\ +10 \\ \hline \end{array}$	8. $\begin{array}{r} 9 \\ +7 \\ \hline \end{array}$	9. $\begin{array}{r} 8 \\ +10 \\ \hline \end{array}$	10. $\begin{array}{r} 6 \\ +10 \\ \hline \end{array}$
11. $\begin{array}{r} 9 \\ +10 \\ \hline \end{array}$	12. $\begin{array}{r} 6 \\ +8 \\ \hline \end{array}$	13. $\begin{array}{r} 8 \\ +8 \\ \hline \end{array}$	14. $\begin{array}{r} 8 \\ +10 \\ \hline \end{array}$	15. $\begin{array}{r} 9 \\ +8 \\ \hline \end{array}$
16. $\begin{array}{r} 9 \\ +7 \\ \hline \end{array}$	17. $\begin{array}{r} 9 \\ +9 \\ \hline \end{array}$	18. $\begin{array}{r} 7 \\ +8 \\ \hline \end{array}$	19. $\begin{array}{r} 10 \\ +7 \\ \hline \end{array}$	20. $\begin{array}{r} 8 \\ +9 \\ \hline \end{array}$
21. $\begin{array}{r} 8 \\ +9 \\ \hline \end{array}$	22. $\begin{array}{r} 9 \\ +9 \\ \hline \end{array}$	23. $\begin{array}{r} 10 \\ +6 \\ \hline \end{array}$	24. $\begin{array}{r} 7 \\ +8 \\ \hline \end{array}$	25. $\begin{array}{r} 8 \\ +7 \\ \hline \end{array}$
26. $\begin{array}{r} 9 \\ +7 \\ \hline \end{array}$	27. $\begin{array}{r} 7 \\ +8 \\ \hline \end{array}$	28. $\begin{array}{r} 9 \\ +6 \\ \hline \end{array}$	29. $\begin{array}{r} 9 \\ +9 \\ \hline \end{array}$	30. $\begin{array}{r} 8 \\ +7 \\ \hline \end{array}$
31. $\begin{array}{r} 6 \\ +7 \\ \hline \end{array}$	32. $\begin{array}{r} 6 \\ +7 \\ \hline \end{array}$	33. $\begin{array}{r} 8 \\ +8 \\ \hline \end{array}$	34. $\begin{array}{r} 10 \\ +9 \\ \hline \end{array}$	35. $\begin{array}{r} 10 \\ +8 \\ \hline \end{array}$
36. $\begin{array}{r} 9 \\ +8 \\ \hline \end{array}$	37. $\begin{array}{r} 9 \\ +8 \\ \hline \end{array}$	38. $\begin{array}{r} 7 \\ +9 \\ \hline \end{array}$	39. $\begin{array}{r} 10 \\ +9 \\ \hline \end{array}$	40. $\begin{array}{r} 6 \\ +10 \\ \hline \end{array}$
41. $\begin{array}{r} 7 \\ +9 \\ \hline \end{array}$	42. $\begin{array}{r} 8 \\ +6 \\ \hline \end{array}$	43. $\begin{array}{r} 8 \\ +7 \\ \hline \end{array}$	44. $\begin{array}{r} 8 \\ +6 \\ \hline \end{array}$	45. $\begin{array}{r} 9 \\ +8 \\ \hline \end{array}$
46. $\begin{array}{r} 8 \\ +10 \\ \hline \end{array}$	47. $\begin{array}{r} 8 \\ +9 \\ \hline \end{array}$	48. $\begin{array}{r} 8 \\ +8 \\ \hline \end{array}$	49. $\begin{array}{r} 7 \\ +7 \\ \hline \end{array}$	50. $\begin{array}{r} 7 \\ +7 \\ \hline \end{array}$

ADDITION 6 TO 10

Name: _____
Date: _____ Time: _____
Score: /50

1. 9
   +7

2. 9
   +8

3. 6
   +8

4. 9
   +8

5. 7
   +8

6. 7
   +10

7. 9
   +9

8. 6
   +7

9. 6
   +9

10. 9
    +9

11. 9
    +10

12. 9
    +9

13. 7
    +9

14. 8
    +9

15. 8
    +7

16. 7
    +10

17. 7
    +7

18. 7
    +6

19. 9
    +7

20. 9
    +8

21. 10
    +8

22. 6
    +9

23. 7
    +8

24. 9
    +8

25. 8
    +7

26. 7
    +9

27. 8
    +8

28. 8
    +9

29. 7
    +8

30. 9
    +7

31. 7
    +6

32. 7
    +7

33. 7
    +8

34. 9
    +6

35. 7
    +10

36. 8
    +6

37. 8
    +9

38. 9
    +9

39. 7
    +8

40. 8
    +7

41. 9
    +6

42. 6
    +8

43. 8
    +9

44. 8
    +7

45. 10
    +9

46. 8
    +7

47. 10
    +8

48. 8
    +9

49. 7
    +8

50. 9
    +7

ADDITION 6 TO 10

1. 9 +8

2. 7 +6

3. 7 +8

4. 10 +9

5. 8 +7

6. 9 +9

7. 8 +7

8. 6 +9

9. 7 +7

10. 9 +9

11. 9 +8

12. 9 +9

13. 9 +10

14. 7 +10

15. 9 +7

16. 8 +7

17. 7 +7

18. 7 +8

19. 6 +10

20. 8 +7

21. 8 +10

22. 7 +7

23. 10 +10

24. 6 +8

25. 8 +8

26. 8 +7

27. 9 +6

28. 9 +6

29. 6 +9

30. 7 +9

31. 9 +7

32. 6 +7

33. 9 +9

34. 10 +10

35. 9 +7

36. 9 +7

37. 8 +7

38. 10 +8

39. 9 +6

40. 8 +8

41. 6 +9

42. 7 +7

43. 8 +8

44. 7 +7

45. 6 +7

46. 7 +9

47. 8 +7

48. 7 +8

49. 10 +10

50. 6 +6

1.	9 +7	2.	8 +7	3.	10 +7	4.	9 +9	5.	7 +8
6.	9 +9	7.	9 +9	8.	10 +6	9.	10 +6	10.	7 +7
11.	7 +9	12.	9 +8	13.	6 +10	14.	9 +8	15.	6 +6
16.	8 +9	17.	6 +9	18.	8 +9	19.	9 +8	20.	9 +7
21.	8 +10	22.	7 +9	23.	10 +8	24.	6 +8	25.	8 +8
26.	7 +9	27.	8 +8	28.	9 +7	29.	8 +7	30.	6 +9
31.	8 +9	32.	7 +7	33.	8 +8	34.	8 +7	35.	10 +9
36.	8 +7	37.	6 +10	38.	6 +9	39.	6 +9	40.	7 +6
41.	7 +10	42.	8 +9	43.	7 +10	44.	7 +8	45.	8 +6
46.	7 +8	47.	8 +9	48.	6 +8	49.	9 +7	50.	8 +6

ADDITION 6 TO 10

Name: _____

Date: _____ Time: _____

Score: /50

1. 9 +8	2. 7 +9	3. 6 +6	4. 6 +7	5. 6 +9
6. 7 +8	7. 8 +8	8. 10 +6	9. 7 +8	10. 6 +7
11. 7 +9	12. 9 +9	13. 8 +9	14. 8 +7	15. 9 +7
16. 9 +8	17. 8 +10	18. 8 +8	19. 8 +7	20. 7 +8
21. 7 +7	22. 6 +8	23. 8 +9	24. 9 +9	25. 9 +7
26. 10 +6	27. 8 +8	28. 8 +7	29. 10 +6	30. 9 +7
31. 10 +8	32. 8 +9	33. 7 +7	34. 7 +8	35. 8 +9
36. 8 +6	37. 9 +7	38. 9 +9	39. 9 +8	40. 7 +6
41. 7 +10	42. 7 +10	43. 9 +9	44. 9 +6	45. 8 +8
46. 9 +7	47. 7 +8	48. 7 +7	49. 9 +8	50. 8 +7

prepaze

www.prepaze.com

ADDITION 6 TO 10

1. 7
   +6

2. 7
   +7

3. 8
   +8

4. 10
   +9

5. 8
   +7

6. 8
   +8

7. 6
   +8

8. 8
   +7

9. 8
   +9

10. 9
    +9

11. 9
    +7

12. 9
    +9

13. 9
    +6

14. 9
    +8

15. 8
    +9

16. 9
    +7

17. 10
    +9

18. 8
    +10

19. 6
    +10

20. 9
    +6

21. 8
    +9

22. 7
    +8

23. 8
    +7

24. 9
    +7

25. 7
    +6

26. 7
    +6

27. 8
    +9

28. 9
    +7

29. 8
    +8

30. 10
    +10

31. 10
    +7

32. 7
    +8

33. 7
    +8

34. 9
    +7

35. 8
    +10

36. 9
    +10

37. 6
    +6

38. 9
    +8

39. 8
    +8

40. 8
    +7

41. 9
    +10

42. 8
    +9

43. 8
    +6

44. 7
    +9

45. 9
    +7

46. 7
    +8

47. 10
    +7

48. 10
    +9

49. 9
    +7

50. 9
    +7

ADDITION 6 TO 10

1. $\begin{array}{r}10\\+8\\\hline\end{array}$	2. $\begin{array}{r}8\\+10\\\hline\end{array}$	3. $\begin{array}{r}6\\+10\\\hline\end{array}$	4. $\begin{array}{r}7\\+6\\\hline\end{array}$	5. $\begin{array}{r}9\\+8\\\hline\end{array}$
6. $\begin{array}{r}6\\+10\\\hline\end{array}$	7. $\begin{array}{r}8\\+9\\\hline\end{array}$	8. $\begin{array}{r}8\\+9\\\hline\end{array}$	9. $\begin{array}{r}8\\+9\\\hline\end{array}$	10. $\begin{array}{r}8\\+9\\\hline\end{array}$
11. $\begin{array}{r}7\\+7\\\hline\end{array}$	12. $\begin{array}{r}7\\+10\\\hline\end{array}$	13. $\begin{array}{r}7\\+9\\\hline\end{array}$	14. $\begin{array}{r}9\\+8\\\hline\end{array}$	15. $\begin{array}{r}7\\+6\\\hline\end{array}$
16. $\begin{array}{r}7\\+8\\\hline\end{array}$	17. $\begin{array}{r}8\\+9\\\hline\end{array}$	18. $\begin{array}{r}7\\+8\\\hline\end{array}$	19. $\begin{array}{r}9\\+7\\\hline\end{array}$	20. $\begin{array}{r}7\\+6\\\hline\end{array}$
21. $\begin{array}{r}6\\+9\\\hline\end{array}$	22. $\begin{array}{r}7\\+7\\\hline\end{array}$	23. $\begin{array}{r}9\\+6\\\hline\end{array}$	24. $\begin{array}{r}8\\+7\\\hline\end{array}$	25. $\begin{array}{r}10\\+8\\\hline\end{array}$
26. $\begin{array}{r}10\\+9\\\hline\end{array}$	27. $\begin{array}{r}7\\+7\\\hline\end{array}$	28. $\begin{array}{r}7\\+8\\\hline\end{array}$	29. $\begin{array}{r}7\\+8\\\hline\end{array}$	30. $\begin{array}{r}7\\+9\\\hline\end{array}$
31. $\begin{array}{r}6\\+8\\\hline\end{array}$	32. $\begin{array}{r}8\\+7\\\hline\end{array}$	33. $\begin{array}{r}7\\+7\\\hline\end{array}$	34. $\begin{array}{r}9\\+6\\\hline\end{array}$	35. $\begin{array}{r}9\\+9\\\hline\end{array}$
36. $\begin{array}{r}7\\+8\\\hline\end{array}$	37. $\begin{array}{r}9\\+8\\\hline\end{array}$	38. $\begin{array}{r}7\\+6\\\hline\end{array}$	39. $\begin{array}{r}9\\+10\\\hline\end{array}$	40. $\begin{array}{r}10\\+8\\\hline\end{array}$
41. $\begin{array}{r}7\\+7\\\hline\end{array}$	42. $\begin{array}{r}6\\+10\\\hline\end{array}$	43. $\begin{array}{r}7\\+8\\\hline\end{array}$	44. $\begin{array}{r}7\\+7\\\hline\end{array}$	45. $\begin{array}{r}9\\+7\\\hline\end{array}$
46. $\begin{array}{r}9\\+6\\\hline\end{array}$	47. $\begin{array}{r}9\\+8\\\hline\end{array}$	48. $\begin{array}{r}7\\+8\\\hline\end{array}$	49. $\begin{array}{r}9\\+8\\\hline\end{array}$	50. $\begin{array}{r}8\\+7\\\hline\end{array}$

FIND THE 10 DIFFERENCES

prepaze

WORD PROBLEMS
ADDITION 6 TO 10

1. Norman has 5 big stickers on his suitcase and 2 small stickers. How many stickers does Norman have altogether?

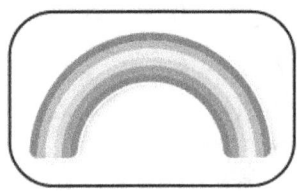

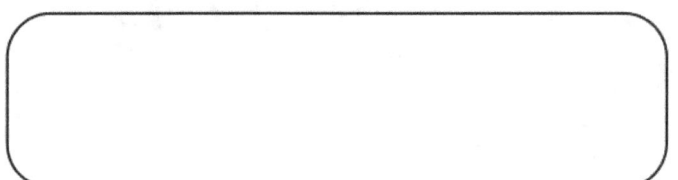

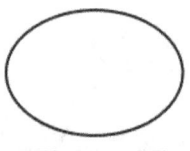

ANSWER

2. There are 7 tables on the left and 3 tables on the right. How many tables are there in all?

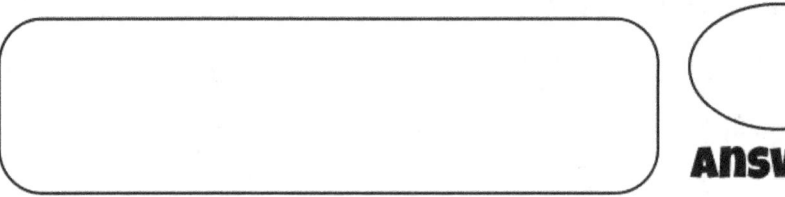

ANSWER

3. Kevin has 4 markers, and Lenny has 4 markers. How many markers do they have altogether?

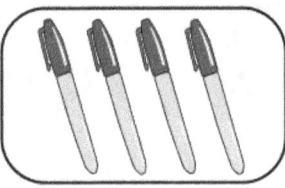

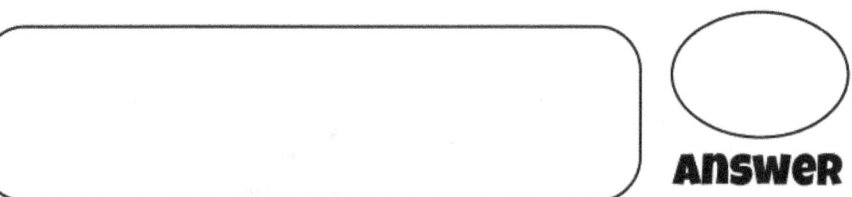

ANSWER

4. A child collects 5 small pebbles and 4 big pebbles. How many pebbles does the child have in all?

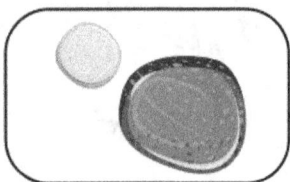

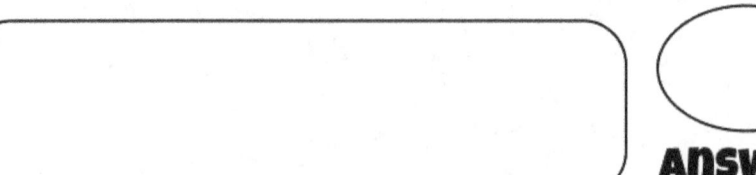

ANSWER

5. Jackie saw 3 kites yesterday. She saw 4 kites today. How many kites did she see altogether?

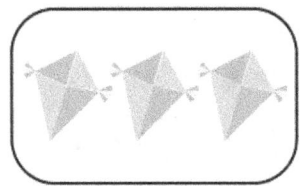

ANSWER

6. 4 children plant trees. 2 more children join them. How many children are there now?

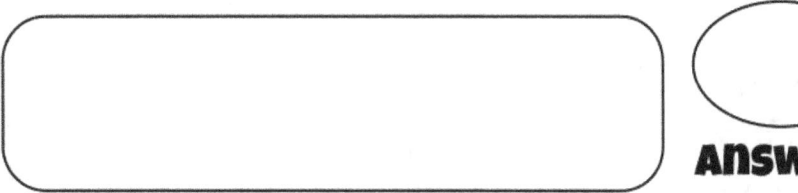

ANSWER

7. Barry has 3 balloons. He finds 5 more balloons. How many balloons does he have altogether?

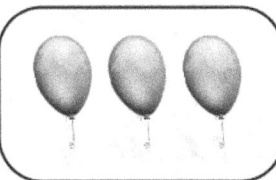
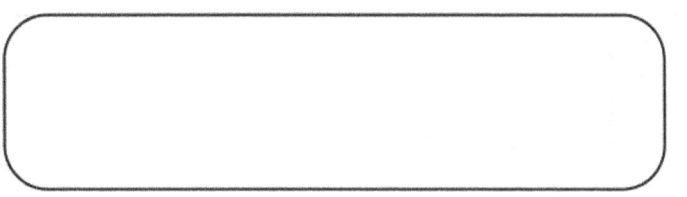

ANSWER

8. Amanda has 6 crayons. Leon has 4 crayons. How many crayons do they have altogether?

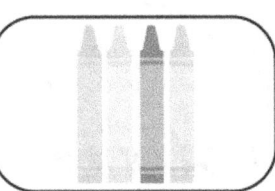

ANSWER

WORD PROBLEMS
ADDITION 6 TO 10

9. There are 5 boys and 4 girls on my team. How many children are there on my team?

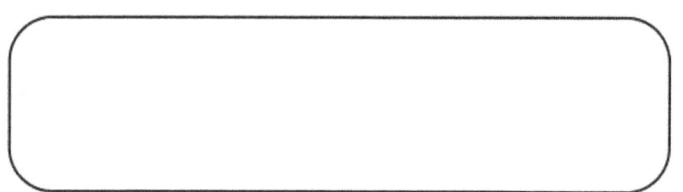

ANSWER

10. Morgan baked 4 cookies. Then he baked 3 more cookies. How many cookies did he bake?

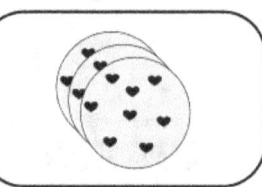

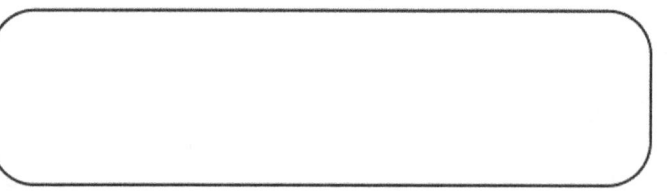

ANSWER

11. There are 3 benches on the left and 3 benches on the right. How many benches are there altogether?

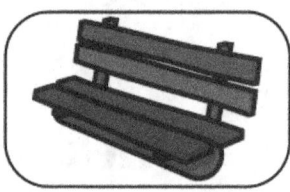

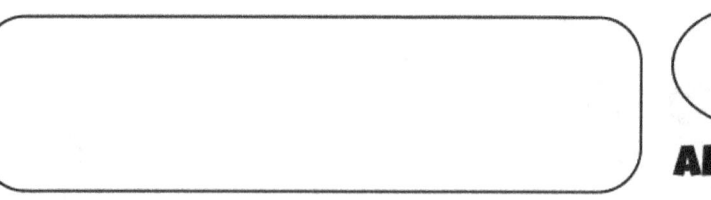

ANSWER

12. There are 5 flowers in a vase and 3 flowers in another vase. How many flowers are there in all?

ANSWER

WORD PROBLEMS
ADDITION 6 TO 10

Name: _____

Date: _____ Time: _____

13. 5 children volunteered to clean up the beach. 5 more children joined them. How many children are cleaning the beach?

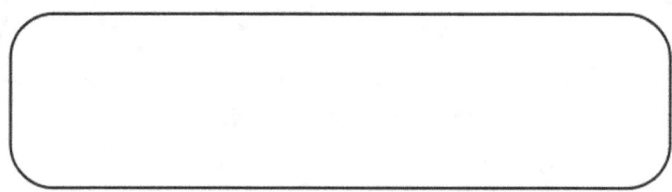

ANSWER

14. We ordered 6 pizzas. Then, we ordered 2 more. How many pizzas did we order?

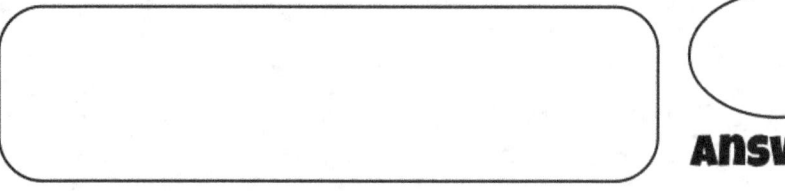

ANSWER

15. Darla has 1 paintbrush. She buys 5 more brushes. How many brushes does she have now?

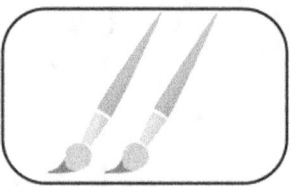

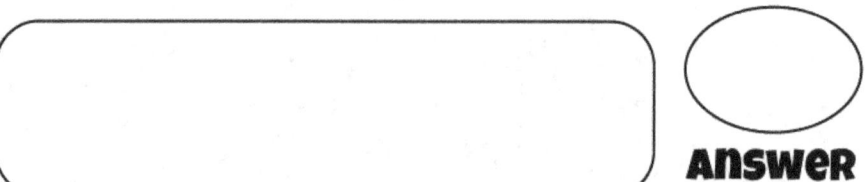

ANSWER

16. Wendy colors 3 rectangles and 4 squares. How many shapes does she color in all?

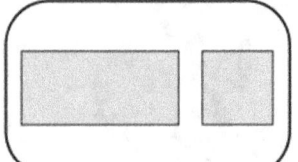

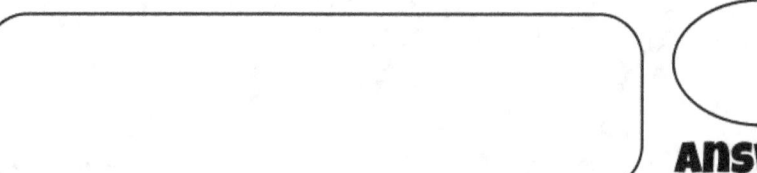

ANSWER

Name: _____

Date: _____ Time: _____

17. Joey has 7 shirts. His friends give him 3 more shirts. How many shirts does he have?

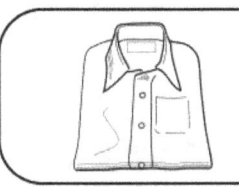 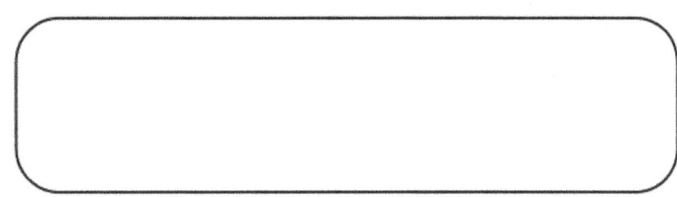

answer

18. Tracy sees 4 ants. Then, she sees 5 more ants join them. How many ants does she see?

 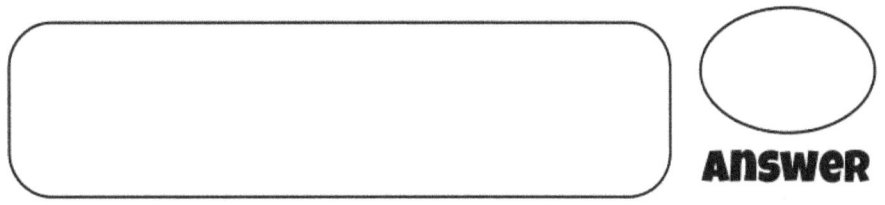

answer

19. Sheldon makes 2 snowballs. Then, he makes 7 more snowballs. How many snowballs does he make altogether?

 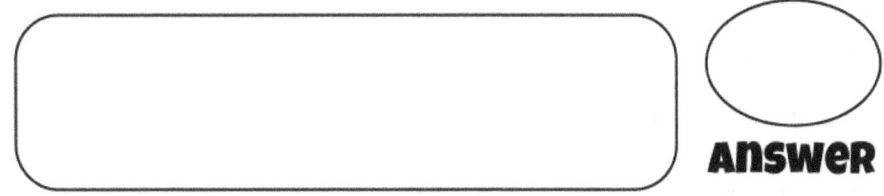

answer

20. Martha breaks 4 bricks, and Sean breaks 3 bricks in martial arts class. How many bricks do they break altogether?

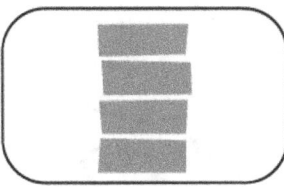 

answer

prepaze

WORD PROBLEMS
ADDITION 6 TO 10

Name: _____
Date: _____ Time: _____

21. Andy peels 3 potatoes, and Penny peels 3 potatoes. How many potatoes do they peel altogether?

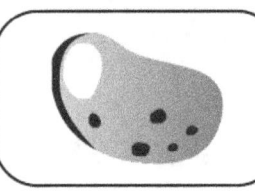

ANSWER

22. Carl makes 4 cards, and Riley makes 4 cards. How many cards do they make?

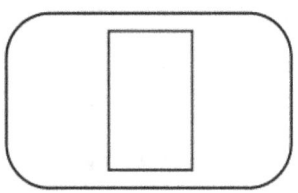

ANSWER

23. Abby has 3 boxes. Dennis has 6 boxes. How many boxes do they have altogether?

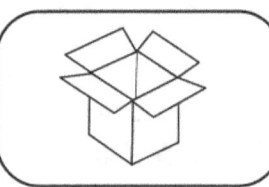

ANSWER

24. George draws 5 circles. Then, he draws another 5 circles. How many circles does he draw?

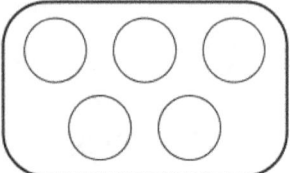

ANSWER

25. 4 people are at a party. 5 more people join them. How many people are at the party now?

answer

ACTIVITY CORNER

CONNECT THE DOTS

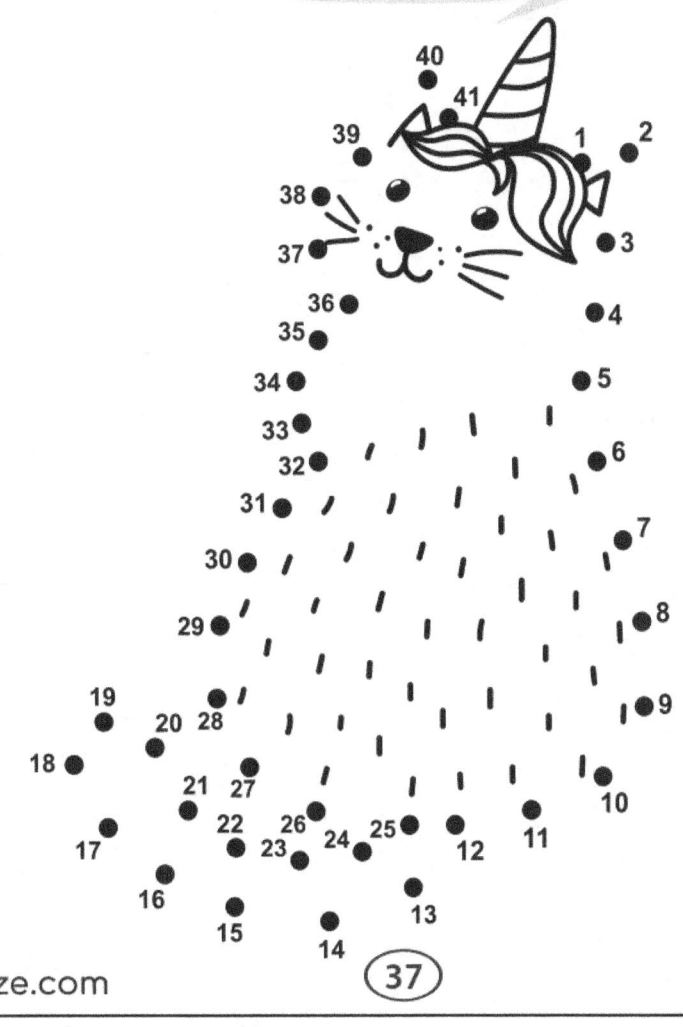

ADDITION 11 TO 15

1. 13 +13	2. 12 +13	3. 12 +13	4. 11 +12	5. 14 +14
6. 14 +13	7. 13 +14	8. 13 +15	9. 12 +14	10. 15 +12
11. 12 +13	12. 14 +14	13. 14 +14	14. 13 +15	15. 11 +14
16. 13 +11	17. 14 +13	18. 14 +15	19. 14 +14	20. 12 +12
21. 14 +14	22. 14 +12	23. 11 +13	24. 14 +14	25. 14 +12
26. 12 +13	27. 13 +13	28. 15 +11	29. 15 +11	30. 14 +14
31. 13 +13	32. 14 +13	33. 15 +14	34. 12 +15	35. 14 +11
36. 12 +13	37. 12 +15	38. 12 +15	39. 14 +15	40. 14 +11
41. 14 +12	42. 14 +11	43. 13 +14	44. 14 +12	45. 15 +15
46. 15 +12	47. 13 +13	48. 11 +11	49. 15 +14	50. 13 +13

ADDITION 11 TO 15

Name: _____

Date: _____ Time: _____

Score: /50

1.	15 +15	2.	11 +14	3.	14 +13	4.	15 +11	5.	13 +11
6.	14 +13	7.	12 +14	8.	12 +14	9.	12 +13	10.	12 +13
11.	15 +12	12.	12 +12	13.	11 +13	14.	12 +12	15.	12 +12
16.	12 +11	17.	14 +14	18.	13 +15	19.	11 +11	20.	12 +15
21.	12 +12	22.	14 +11	23.	11 +12	24.	15 +12	25.	11 +13
26.	14 +14	27.	14 +11	28.	15 +15	29.	12 +15	30.	12 +13
31.	14 +12	32.	12 +13	33.	12 +13	34.	11 +12	35.	12 +12
36.	14 +11	37.	12 +14	38.	13 +14	39.	14 +12	40.	12 +14
41.	12 +11	42.	15 +14	43.	13 +13	44.	14 +11	45.	15 +12
46.	12 +11	47.	14 +13	48.	14 +13	49.	14 +14	50.	14 +12

prepaze

1. 12 +13	2. 13 +14	3. 11 +13	4. 12 +12	5. 12 +14
6. 13 +15	7. 12 +15	8. 12 +12	9. 13 +11	10. 12 +13
11. 15 +14	12. 13 +12	13. 11 +11	14. 11 +14	15. 11 +12
16. 13 +13	17. 12 +11	18. 14 +14	19. 14 +12	20. 12 +13
21. 12 +15	22. 14 +13	23. 12 +14	24. 13 +11	25. 13 +13
26. 12 +14	27. 11 +12	28. 13 +15	29. 14 +12	30. 14 +14
31. 11 +15	32. 13 +12	33. 15 +13	34. 14 +12	35. 14 +14
36. 11 +14	37. 13 +14	38. 12 +12	39. 12 +14	40. 15 +13
41. 12 +12	42. 14 +14	43. 15 +14	44. 14 +15	45. 14 +12
46. 12 +14	47. 11 +14	48. 14 +11	49. 14 +14	50. 12 +14

ADDITION 11 TO 15

1.	11 +12	2.	14 +14	3.	14 +12	4.	13 +12	5.	12 +12
6.	12 +15	7.	13 +15	8.	12 +12	9.	12 +13	10.	15 +14
11.	12 +14	12.	14 +12	13.	14 +14	14.	13 +12	15.	14 +12
16.	14 +13	17.	14 +14	18.	12 +11	19.	13 +13	20.	14 +12
21.	14 +14	22.	13 +11	23.	14 +14	24.	13 +13	25.	12 +13
26.	14 +14	27.	13 +13	28.	15 +15	29.	14 +13	30.	12 +15
31.	15 +14	32.	13 +15	33.	14 +12	34.	13 +14	35.	12 +15
36.	13 +13	37.	13 +13	38.	13 +12	39.	13 +15	40.	13 +13
41.	11 +11	42.	13 +12	43.	11 +14	44.	13 +13	45.	14 +12
46.	11 +11	47.	11 +11	48.	13 +13	49.	14 +14	50.	13 +14

1. 12 +12	2. 12 +13	3. 14 +11	4. 15 +15	5. 14 +11
6. 14 +13	7. 11 +13	8. 14 +14	9. 11 +14	10. 13 +13
11. 15 +14	12. 15 +11	13. 13 +13	14. 14 +13	15. 14 +14
16. 13 +11	17. 12 +12	18. 14 +15	19. 13 +12	20. 11 +14
21. 12 +14	22. 13 +14	23. 13 +14	24. 11 +14	25. 12 +12
26. 13 +13	27. 12 +13	28. 11 +12	29. 11 +12	30. 15 +14
31. 12 +13	32. 14 +13	33. 13 +14	34. 12 +15	35. 12 +12
36. 13 +12	37. 12 +13	38. 13 +13	39. 12 +15	40. 12 +12
41. 14 +14	42. 12 +11	43. 11 +14	44. 15 +13	45. 12 +12
46. 14 +14	47. 14 +13	48. 14 +11	49. 11 +15	50. 14 +13

ADDITION 11 TO 15

Name: _____
Date: _____ Time: _____
Score: /50

1.	11 +12	2.	14 +13	3.	11 +11	4.	12 +12	5.	11 +15
6.	11 +11	7.	12 +14	8.	15 +12	9.	13 +13	10.	12 +11
11.	12 +12	12.	11 +13	13.	12 +14	14.	11 +13	15.	15 +15
16.	14 +11	17.	13 +12	18.	15 +13	19.	14 +14	20.	13 +12
21.	12 +14	22.	14 +12	23.	13 +11	24.	13 +14	25.	12 +13
26.	13 +11	27.	12 +13	28.	12 +15	29.	13 +14	30.	13 +15
31.	13 +14	32.	14 +12	33.	12 +14	34.	13 +13	35.	14 +14
36.	13 +14	37.	12 +15	38.	11 +12	39.	11 +15	40.	12 +15
41.	14 +13	42.	11 +14	43.	13 +12	44.	12 +12	45.	12 +14
46.	13 +11	47.	14 +14	48.	13 +11	49.	12 +13	50.	11 +13

ADDITION 11 TO 15

1.	12 +14	2.	14 +13	3.	11 +11	4.	14 +12	5.	12 +12
6.	11 +14	7.	13 +13	8.	14 +12	9.	15 +14	10.	13 +13
11.	14 +14	12.	12 +13	13.	15 +12	14.	13 +14	15.	13 +14
16.	14 +13	17.	13 +12	18.	13 +13	19.	13 +12	20.	11 +13
21.	14 +13	22.	13 +13	23.	12 +12	24.	12 +12	25.	13 +11
26.	12 +15	27.	14 +11	28.	14 +13	29.	12 +11	30.	13 +13
31.	14 +14	32.	13 +13	33.	12 +13	34.	13 +12	35.	14 +14
36.	14 +11	37.	12 +12	38.	15 +13	39.	13 +13	40.	14 +12
41.	13 +15	42.	13 +12	43.	12 +14	44.	14 +11	45.	11 +11
46.	14 +13	47.	12 +14	48.	11 +12	49.	13 +12	50.	14 +13

| 1. | 11 +13 | 2. | 13 +12 | 3. | 12 +12 | 4. | 12 +13 | 5. | 15 +14 |

| 6. | 11 +12 | 7. | 15 +11 | 8. | 13 +13 | 9. | 13 +14 | 10. | 14 +13 |

| 11. | 13 +13 | 12. | 14 +13 | 13. | 13 +12 | 14. | 13 +12 | 15. | 13 +13 |

| 16. | 14 +14 | 17. | 14 +13 | 18. | 14 +14 | 19. | 14 +11 | 20. | 15 +13 |

| 21. | 15 +12 | 22. | 12 +13 | 23. | 14 +14 | 24. | 13 +13 | 25. | 12 +13 |

| 26. | 12 +13 | 27. | 14 +12 | 28. | 12 +15 | 29. | 14 +13 | 30. | 11 +13 |

| 31. | 12 +13 | 32. | 13 +14 | 33. | 12 +12 | 34. | 13 +11 | 35. | 13 +14 |

| 36. | 12 +14 | 37. | 14 +11 | 38. | 12 +13 | 39. | 15 +14 | 40. | 13 +14 |

| 41. | 11 +13 | 42. | 12 +12 | 43. | 13 +13 | 44. | 11 +11 | 45. | 13 +14 |

| 46. | 12 +13 | 47. | 12 +12 | 48. | 11 +13 | 49. | 12 +11 | 50. | 13 +14 |

ACTIVITY CORNER

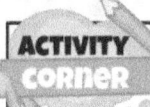

Sum of Numbers

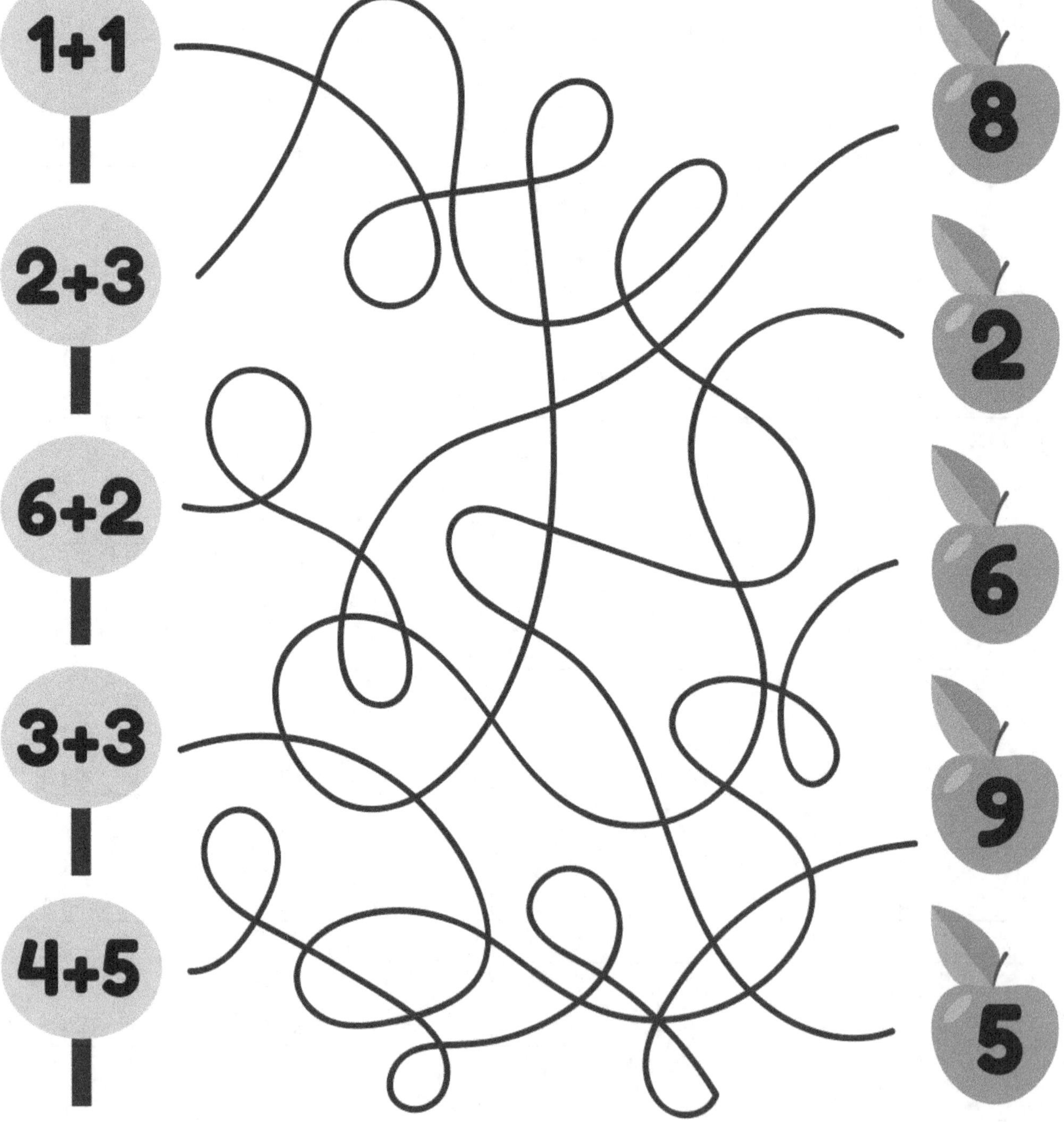
1+1
2+3
6+2
3+3
4+5
8
2
6
9
5

WORD PROBLEMS
ADDITION 11 TO 15

Name: _____
Date: _____ Time: _____

1. Jane takes 3 pears out of the fridge. There are 8 pears left in the refrigerator. How many pears does she have altogether?

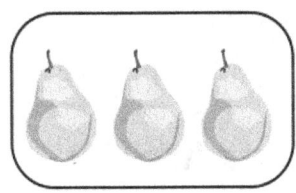

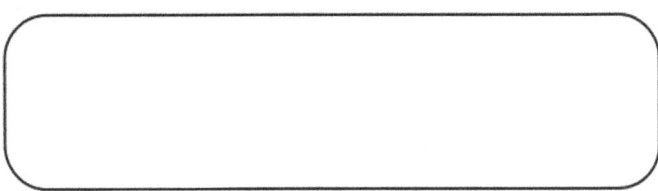

ANSWER

2. Harry stacks a can of length 5 inches and a bottle that is 8 inches long. What is the total length?

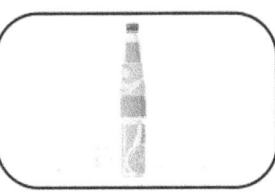

ANSWER

3. Wilma has 5 coins. Her sister gives her 10 more coins. How many coins does she have now?

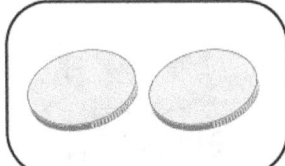

ANSWER

4. Tom has 7 balls. Sofia has 7 balls. How many balls do they have altogether?

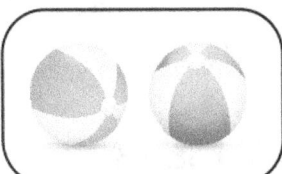

ANSWER

WORD PROBLEMS
ADDITION 11 TO 15

5. Erika has 5 friends. She makes 7 new friends. How many friends does Erika have now?

ANSWER

6. Jonah makes 5 pancakes for him. Then he makes 9 more pancakes for others. How many pancakes does he make?

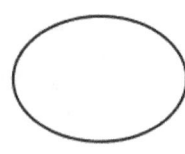
ANSWER

7. Zoey makes 6 small paper boats and 5 big paper boats. How many paper boats does she make?

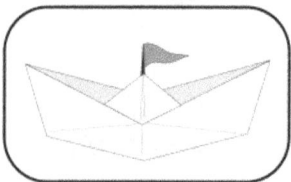

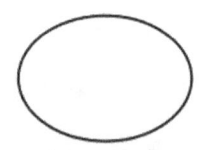
ANSWER

8. Ryan has a collection of 11 pens. His father gives him 4 more pens. How many pens does he have now?

ANSWER

WORD PROBLEMS
ADDITION 11 TO 15

Name: _____
Date: _____ Time: _____

9. Gavin has 9 games on his laptop. He installs 4 more games. How many games does he have now?

ANSWER

10. Anna gave her elder sister 6 bows and gave her younger sister 6 bows. How many bows did she give away?

ANSWER

11. Riley sees 3 ducks on the land and sees 11 ducks in the pond. How many birds does Riley see?

ANSWER

12. Bella cuts a wire into 6 pieces. Then she cuts another wire into 5 pieces. How many pieces of wires does she have now?

ANSWER

COLORING ACTIVITY

WORD PROBLEMS
ADDITION 11 TO 15

13. Eli catches 7 fish on Saturday and 8 fish on Sunday. How many fish does he catch in 2 days?

ANSWER

14. Justin read 4 story books this week and 9 story books the previous week. How many story books has he read in two weeks?

 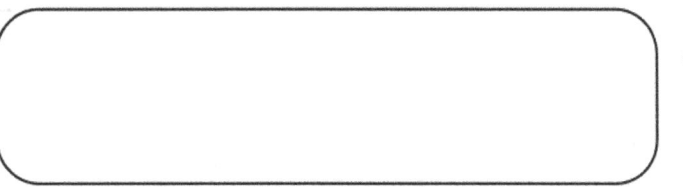 

ANSWER

15. Molly has 3 formal skirts and 12 informal skirts. How many skirts does she have?

  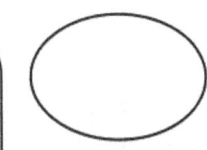

ANSWER

16. Eden wrote 6 poems this month and 8 poems the previous month. How many poems has he written by far?

ANSWER

Name: _____

Date: _____ Time: _____

17. There is a pile of 7 sticks. Cole adds 5 more sticks to the pile. How many sticks are there now?

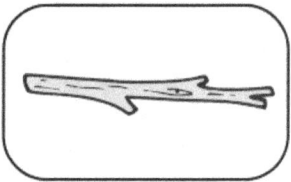

ANSWER

18. 9 of Jade's arrows hit the target, and 4 of the arrows missed the target. How many arrows did Jade release?

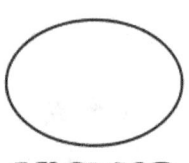

ANSWER

19. There are 4 color pencils in a cup. We add 10 more color pencils. How many color pencils are there now?

ANSWER

20. Today, Lyla learned 8 new words at school and 7 new words at home. How many words did Lyla learn today?

ANSWER

WORD PROBLEMS
ADDITION 11 TO 15

Name: _____
Date: _____ Time: _____

21. Grant has 9 stamps. He buys 2 more stamps. How many stamps does he have now?

ANSWER

22. Eden has 5 ribbons and Sam has 7 ribbons. How many ribbons do they have in all?

ANSWER

23. Oliver places 6 oranges on a tray and 8 oranges in another tray. How many oranges are there altogether?

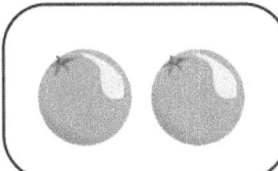

ANSWER

24. Troy has 6 thumbtacks, and Cody has 7 thumbtacks. How many thumbtacks do they have altogether?

ANSWER

prepaze

WORD PROBLEMS
ADDITION 11 TO 15

25. Ariel fed 10 fish in a fish tank and 5 fish in another fish tank. How many fish did Ariel feed?

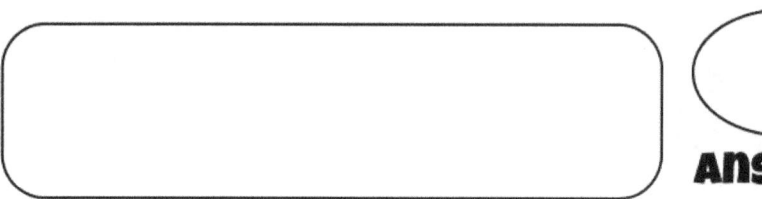

ANSWER

CONNECT THE DOTS

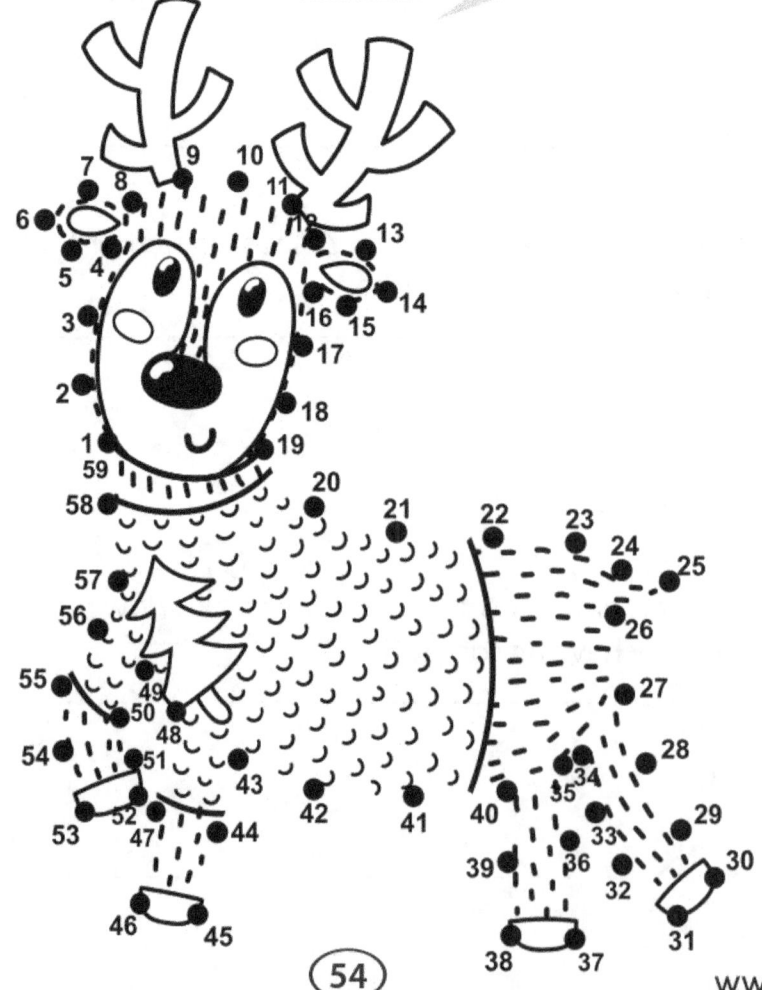

ADDITION 0 TO 15

1. $\begin{array}{r} 2 \\ +6 \\ \hline \end{array}$	2. $\begin{array}{r} 1 \\ +4 \\ \hline \end{array}$	3. $\begin{array}{r} 11 \\ +1 \\ \hline \end{array}$	4. $\begin{array}{r} 11 \\ +6 \\ \hline \end{array}$	5. $\begin{array}{r} 2 \\ +14 \\ \hline \end{array}$
6. $\begin{array}{r} 9 \\ +13 \\ \hline \end{array}$	7. $\begin{array}{r} 12 \\ +12 \\ \hline \end{array}$	8. $\begin{array}{r} 11 \\ +11 \\ \hline \end{array}$	9. $\begin{array}{r} 11 \\ +2 \\ \hline \end{array}$	10. $\begin{array}{r} 13 \\ +13 \\ \hline \end{array}$
11. $\begin{array}{r} 1 \\ +12 \\ \hline \end{array}$	12. $\begin{array}{r} 11 \\ +6 \\ \hline \end{array}$	13. $\begin{array}{r} 15 \\ +9 \\ \hline \end{array}$	14. $\begin{array}{r} 4 \\ +4 \\ \hline \end{array}$	15. $\begin{array}{r} 3 \\ +2 \\ \hline \end{array}$
16. $\begin{array}{r} 10 \\ +3 \\ \hline \end{array}$	17. $\begin{array}{r} 7 \\ +1 \\ \hline \end{array}$	18. $\begin{array}{r} 12 \\ +6 \\ \hline \end{array}$	19. $\begin{array}{r} 6 \\ +5 \\ \hline \end{array}$	20. $\begin{array}{r} 5 \\ +4 \\ \hline \end{array}$
21. $\begin{array}{r} 10 \\ +8 \\ \hline \end{array}$	22. $\begin{array}{r} 14 \\ +13 \\ \hline \end{array}$	23. $\begin{array}{r} 4 \\ +9 \\ \hline \end{array}$	24. $\begin{array}{r} 14 \\ +7 \\ \hline \end{array}$	25. $\begin{array}{r} 2 \\ +10 \\ \hline \end{array}$
26. $\begin{array}{r} 11 \\ +10 \\ \hline \end{array}$	27. $\begin{array}{r} 13 \\ +3 \\ \hline \end{array}$	28. $\begin{array}{r} 8 \\ +3 \\ \hline \end{array}$	29. $\begin{array}{r} 0 \\ +10 \\ \hline \end{array}$	30. $\begin{array}{r} 2 \\ +6 \\ \hline \end{array}$
31. $\begin{array}{r} 13 \\ +7 \\ \hline \end{array}$	32. $\begin{array}{r} 8 \\ +4 \\ \hline \end{array}$	33. $\begin{array}{r} 14 \\ +10 \\ \hline \end{array}$	34. $\begin{array}{r} 3 \\ +4 \\ \hline \end{array}$	35. $\begin{array}{r} 0 \\ +11 \\ \hline \end{array}$
36. $\begin{array}{r} 15 \\ +14 \\ \hline \end{array}$	37. $\begin{array}{r} 11 \\ +8 \\ \hline \end{array}$	38. $\begin{array}{r} 11 \\ +11 \\ \hline \end{array}$	39. $\begin{array}{r} 14 \\ +8 \\ \hline \end{array}$	40. $\begin{array}{r} 10 \\ +15 \\ \hline \end{array}$
41. $\begin{array}{r} 9 \\ +6 \\ \hline \end{array}$	42. $\begin{array}{r} 1 \\ +11 \\ \hline \end{array}$	43. $\begin{array}{r} 13 \\ +13 \\ \hline \end{array}$	44. $\begin{array}{r} 10 \\ +0 \\ \hline \end{array}$	45. $\begin{array}{r} 11 \\ +11 \\ \hline \end{array}$
46. $\begin{array}{r} 12 \\ +6 \\ \hline \end{array}$	47. $\begin{array}{r} 4 \\ +6 \\ \hline \end{array}$	48. $\begin{array}{r} 5 \\ +13 \\ \hline \end{array}$	49. $\begin{array}{r} 7 \\ +1 \\ \hline \end{array}$	50. $\begin{array}{r} 10 \\ +10 \\ \hline \end{array}$

ADDITION 0 TO 15

Name: _____

Date: _____ Time: _____

Score: /50

1. 9 +6	2. 9 +1	3. 6 +6	4. 10 +13	5. 3 +2
6. 9 +0	7. 9 +2	8. 5 +13	9. 7 +15	10. 9 +12
11. 5 +7	12. 8 +7	13. 1 +12	14. 5 +9	15. 9 +8
16. 6 +5	17. 10 +1	18. 11 +11	19. 2 +6	20. 14 +7
21. 11 +12	22. 2 +10	23. 3 +7	24. 0 +12	25. 13 +3
26. 1 +12	27. 8 +8	28. 8 +8	29. 12 +14	30. 10 +2
31. 13 +7	32. 0 +11	33. 2 +1	34. 13 +13	35. 0 +11
36. 9 +15	37. 13 +3	38. 9 +2	39. 6 +5	40. 7 +7
41. 14 +5	42. 11 +14	43. 9 +12	44. 3 +3	45. 14 +6
46. 7 +7	47. 12 +7	48. 0 +15	49. 3 +1	50. 5 +2

1.	9 +12	2.	9 +10	3.	14 +6	4.	1 +2	5.	9 +10
6.	4 +9	7.	8 +12	8.	3 +15	9.	13 +11	10.	12 +2
11.	13 +6	12.	12 +11	13.	0 +12	14.	9 +12	15.	13 +5
16.	1 +9	17.	11 +12	18.	13 +13	19.	10 +8	20.	7 +1
21.	5 +6	22.	7 +7	23.	10 +5	24.	1 +10	25.	4 +5
26.	0 +7	27.	14 +12	28.	15 +3	29.	11 +10	30.	10 +4
31.	15 +5	32.	2 +11	33.	10 +13	34.	11 +14	35.	5 +2
36.	8 +9	37.	3 +6	38.	7 +12	39.	2 +7	40.	1 +1
41.	10 +13	42.	2 +13	43.	1 +10	44.	12 +7	45.	3 +7
46.	5 +14	47.	11 +4	48.	13 +2	49.	14 +15	50.	7 +13

ADDITION 0 TO 15

1. 8 +12	2. 6 +10	3. 4 +4	4. 14 +4	5. 11 +7
6. 15 +5	7. 13 +7	8. 3 +9	9. 6 +8	10. 9 +1
11. 7 +6	12. 6 +3	13. 15 +3	14. 1 +4	15. 3 +6
16. 3 +12	17. 10 +1	18. 6 +6	19. 6 +12	20. 14 +11
21. 3 +2	22. 4 +9	23. 14 +5	24. 9 +8	25. 2 +1
26. 5 +0	27. 14 +15	28. 1 +6	29. 1 +2	30. 6 +6
31. 3 +2	32. 3 +4	33. 11 +3	34. 14 +13	35. 3 +0
36. 7 +4	37. 8 +11	38. 7 +0	39. 5 +9	40. 11 +4
41. 1 +4	42. 3 +15	43. 4 +11	44. 2 +12	45. 13 +12
46. 1 +1	47. 14 +5	48. 2 +2	49. 10 +9	50. 6 +2

ADDITION 0 TO 15

Name: _____

Date: _____ Time: _____

Score: /50

1. 9 +4	2. 0 +1	3. 11 +12	4. 0 +8	5. 8 +6
6. 1 +6	7. 12 +11	8. 14 +6	9. 5 +13	10. 7 +11
11. 3 +13	12. 3 +10	13. 2 +10	14. 9 +3	15. 0 +4
16. 6 +8	17. 12 +12	18. 11 +12	19. 14 +13	20. 8 +3
21. 6 +0	22. 9 +1	23. 9 +12	24. 2 +1	25. 14 +4
26. 3 +3	27. 14 +5	28. 7 +14	29. 13 +7	30. 6 +14
31. 11 +11	32. 10 +12	33. 0 +4	34. 5 +12	35. 0 +11
36. 15 +4	37. 11 +9	38. 13 +1	39. 15 +9	40. 3 +12
41. 14 +14	42. 13 +2	43. 6 +10	44. 1 +8	45. 5 +10
46. 2 +4	47. 4 +1	48. 4 +2	49. 12 +1	50. 15 +5

prepaze

1. 3 +2	2. 15 +14	3. 1 +3	4. 0 +9	5. 14 +7
6. 5 +6	7. 12 +1	8. 15 +4	9. 11 +1	10. 14 +6
11. 8 +11	12. 0 +4	13. 9 +7	14. 3 +13	15. 12 +3
16. 3 +4	17. 14 +8	18. 1 +7	19. 10 +4	20. 1 +7
21. 14 +9	22. 9 +0	23. 8 +10	24. 14 +1	25. 15 +11
26. 5 +12	27. 11 +4	28. 9 +6	29. 7 +14	30. 6 +6
31. 1 +8	32. 6 +13	33. 1 +12	34. 8 +14	35. 3 +2
36. 3 +2	37. 12 +1	38. 9 +6	39. 4 +10	40. 8 +14
41. 2 +10	42. 4 +8	43. 8 +13	44. 6 +4	45. 12 +12
46. 6 +11	47. 5 +10	48. 10 +2	49. 8 +5	50. 1 +11

Name: _____

Date: _____ Time: _____

Score: __/50

1. 13 +6	2. 11 +13	3. 2 +3	4. 14 +14	5. 10 +6
6. 8 +9	7. 1 +6	8. 9 +6	9. 8 +10	10. 7 +12
11. 9 +4	12. 8 +2	13. 2 +4	14. 1 +14	15. 6 +1
16. 11 +0	17. 7 +6	18. 6 +11	19. 3 +8	20. 8 +7
21. 7 +2	22. 14 +2	23. 11 +7	24. 3 +11	25. 15 +8
26. 5 +12	27. 2 +2	28. 3 +11	29. 4 +12	30. 13 +12
31. 8 +1	32. 15 +2	33. 10 +12	34. 14 +7	35. 0 +8
36. 14 +11	37. 2 +13	38. 1 +6	39. 2 +1	40. 14 +4
41. 2 +13	42. 13 +3	43. 0 +1	44. 9 +5	45. 4 +2
46. 3 +10	47. 2 +10	48. 10 +11	49. 12 +12	50. 3 +4

prepaze

Name: _____

Date: _____   Time: _____

Score: /50

1.	5 +2	2.	12 +15	3.	5 +2	4.	1 +13	5.	3 +2
6.	1 +13	7.	8 +11	8.	13 +11	9.	6 +12	10.	2 +2
11.	15 +9	12.	7 +11	13.	5 +1	14.	10 +8	15.	3 +5
16.	9 +4	17.	2 +3	18.	7 +1	19.	12 +2	20.	12 +13
21.	4 +7	22.	9 +2	23.	13 +3	24.	0 +13	25.	10 +15
26.	9 +9	27.	15 +4	28.	2 +9	29.	4 +4	30.	9 +0
31.	14 +9	32.	12 +13	33.	7 +12	34.	5 +2	35.	3 +1
36.	6 +10	37.	3 +9	38.	8 +5	39.	10 +6	40.	5 +13
41.	3 +11	42.	14 +13	43.	3 +3	44.	11 +13	45.	13 +6
46.	11 +9	47.	0 +1	48.	6 +9	49.	2 +10	50.	12 +12

WORD PROBLEMS
ADDITION 0 TO 15

Name: _____
Date: _____ Time: _____

1. Paige has an elder brother and a younger sister. How many siblings does Paige have?

ANSWER

2. Bryan has 1 cat. He brought 2 more cats. How many cats does he have now?

 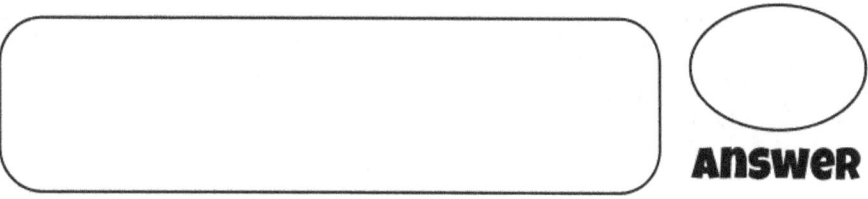

ANSWER

3. Nicole has 3 toy trucks and 2 toy trains. How many toys does she have?

 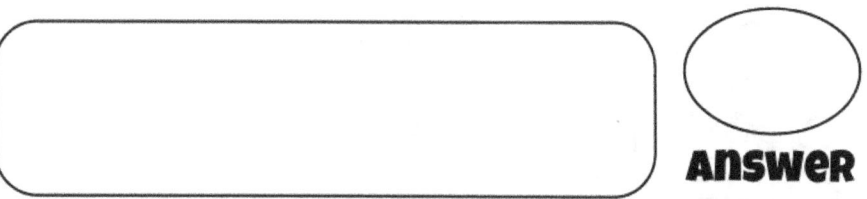

ANSWER

4. There are 2 apple trees and 2 plum trees. How many trees are there?

ANSWER

WORD PROBLEMS
ADDITION 0 TO 15

5. Ivan ate a burger for lunch today and another burger for dinner. How many burgers did he eat today?

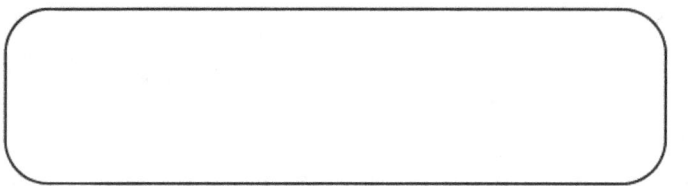

answer

6. Clara has 2 cucumbers and 2 pumpkins. How many vegetables does Clara have?

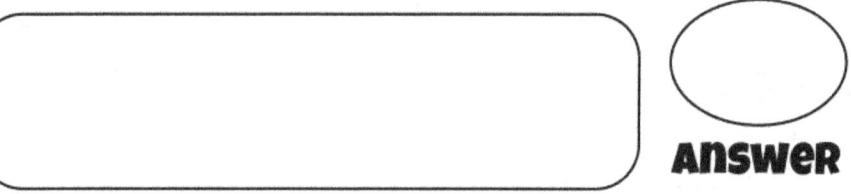

answer

7. Alan has 3 hamsters and 2 spiders. How many pets does Alan have?

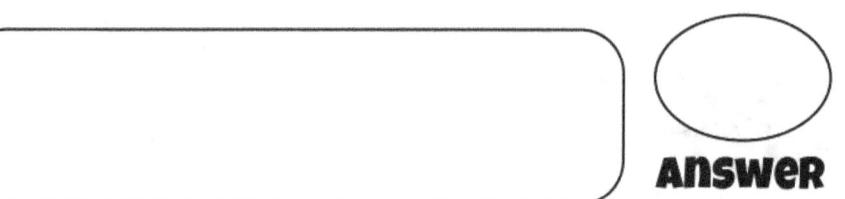

answer

8. Mila ate 2 donuts. Then she ate another donut. How many donuts did Mila eat?

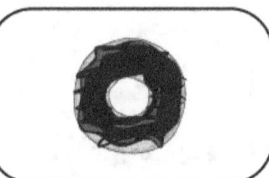

answer

WORD PROBLEMS
ADDITION 0 TO 15

9. Derek has 2 markers, and Sandy has 4 markers. How many markers do they have altogether?

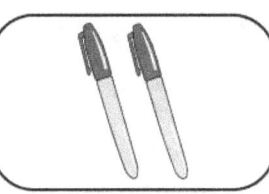

ANSWER

10. Quinn ate 4 plums and her sister ate 4 plums. How many plums did they eat in all ?

ANSWER

11. There are 5 chairs on the left and 2 chairs on the right. How many chairs are there?

ANSWER

12. Collin rang the bell 6 times. Then, he rang it 4 more times. How many times did he ring the bell?

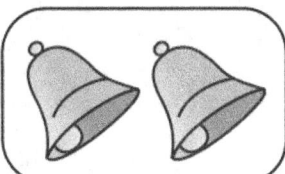

ANSWER

ADD THE NUMBERS

10 + 5 =

12 + 13 =

15 + 9 =

2 + 8 =

WORD PROBLEMS
ADDITION 0 TO 15

Name: _____

Date: _____ Time: _____

13. Angel helped her mom for 5 days. Then she helped her dad for 4 days. How many days did she help her parents?

ANSWER

14. Ezra sings 3 songs in the morning and 5 songs in the evening. How many songs does Ezra sing in a day?

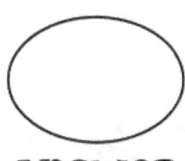
ANSWER

15. Cora has 3 big shells and 3 small shells. How many shells does she have?

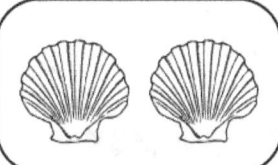

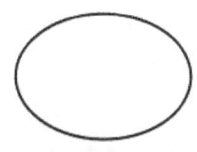
ANSWER

16. Zane has 2 cookies. He baked 5 more cookies. How many cookies does he have?

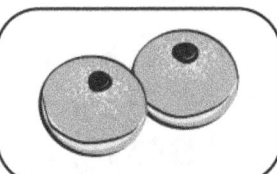

ANSWER

WORD PROBLEMS
ADDITION 0 TO 15

Name: _____
Date: _____ Time: _____

17. Erin makes 5 paper cranes and 6 paper fishes. How many animals does she make in all?

ANSWER

18. Andre has 3 hard candies and 9 candy corns. How many candies does he have?

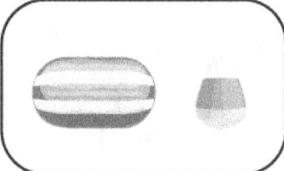  

ANSWER

19. There are 6 children in the park. 8 more children join them. How many children are in the park now?

 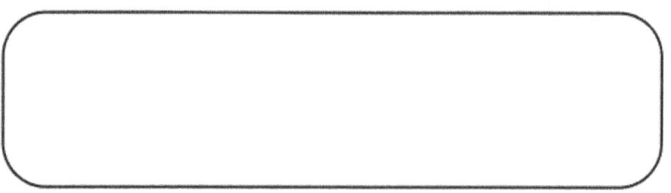 

ANSWER

20. Lola draws 10 squares and 3 triangles. How many shapes does she draw?

ANSWER

WORD PROBLEMS
ADDITION 0 TO 15

Name: _____
Date: _____ Time: _____

21. Tyson has 5 balloons. Amy has 10 balloons. How many balloons do they have altogether?

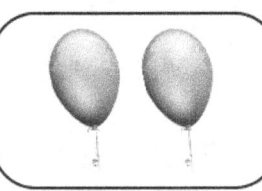

ANSWER

22. Lexi saw 5 horses and Jane saw 7 horses. How many horses did they see altogether?

ANSWER

23. Luca made 6 paintings last week and 7 paintings this week. How many paintings did he make?

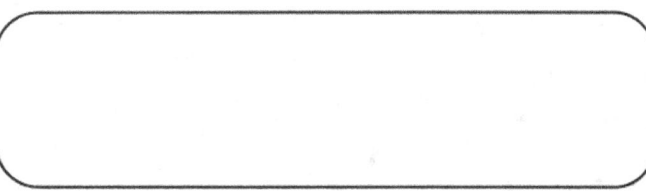

ANSWER

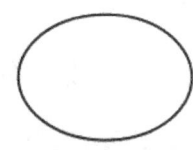

24. Kyla worked for 9 hours and Rob worked for 5 hours. How many hours did they work altogether?

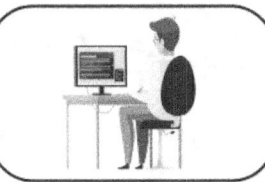

ANSWER

WORD PROBLEMS
ADDITION 0 TO 15

Name: ____________________
Date: __________ Time: __________

25. Finn ran 8 miles in two days and Anna ran 7 miles in two days. How many miles did they run altogether?

Answer

ACTIVITY CORNER

FIND A WAY

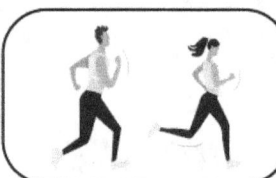

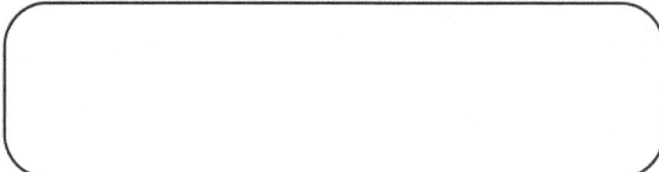

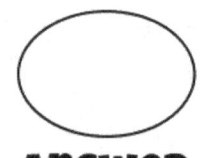

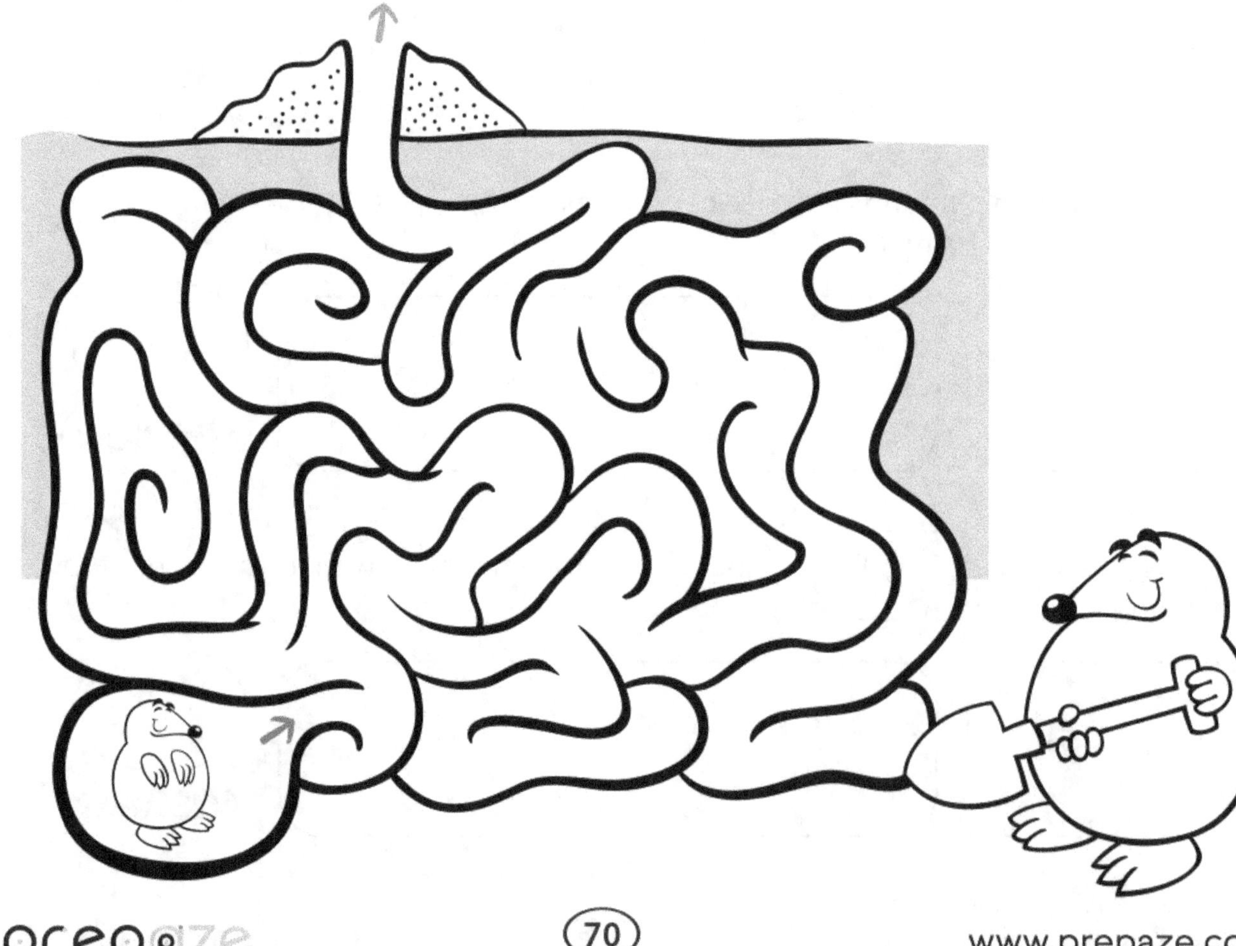

HELLO EVERYONE!

Let's learn
math with

SUBTRACTION

Shall we start?
Let's go!

SUBTRACTION

The process of taking away a quantity from another quantity is called subtraction. Subtraction is one of the four basic operations of arithmetic. The symbol used to represent subtraction is ", commonly known as minus.

When we subtract, the number of things in the group reduce or become less.

Example:

3 - 1 = 2

To subtract 2 from 3, we can count backward 2 steps from 3.

Which can be represented in number line as follows,

2. Count backward as many

times the second the number.

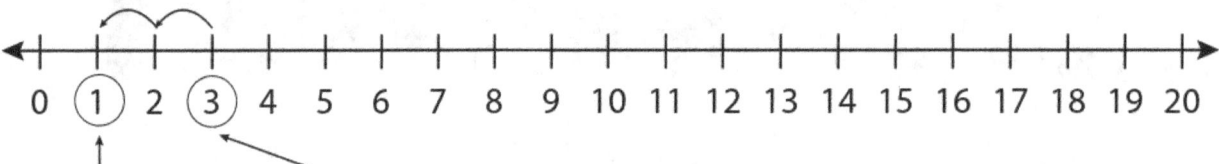

0 1 2 3 4 5 6 7 8 9 10 11 12 13 14 15 16 17 18 19 20

1. Start from the   3. The number

big number   reached is the answer

A subtraction sentence is a mathematical expression that shows the quantities subtracted and their difference.

3 - 2 = 1

We can write the mathematical expression for 12 minus 8 equals 4 as:

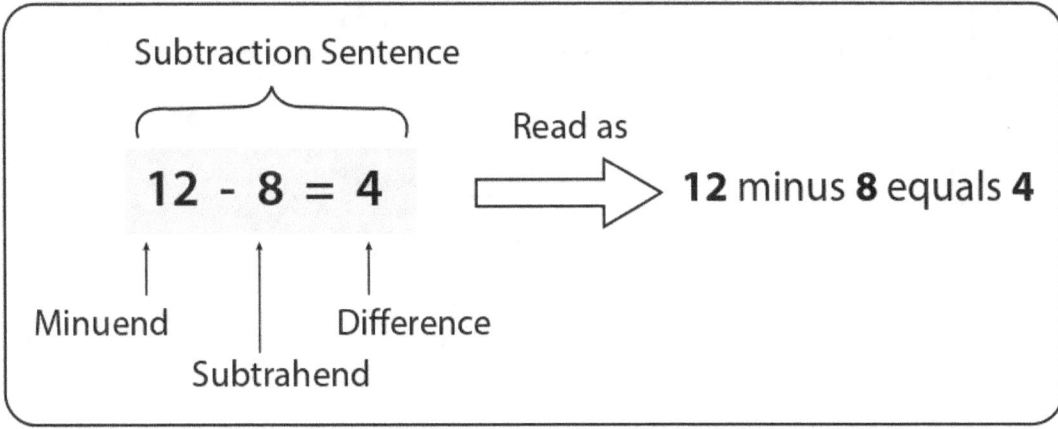

Subtraction Sentence

$$12 - 8 = 4$$

Read as $\Rightarrow$ **12** minus **8** equals **4**

Minuend

Subtrahend

Difference

The minuend, subtrahend, and difference are parts of a subtraction problem. In the subtraction problem, $9 - 5 = 4$, the number 9 is the minuend, the number 5 is the subtrahend and the number 4 is the difference.

Subtraction is the opposite of addition and every addition problem can be rewritten as a subtraction problem.

10 - 7 = 3

SUBTRACTION 0 TO 5

1.	3 −0	2.	4 −0	3.	3 −1	4.	3 −1	5.	2 −1
6.	1 −0	7.	2 −2	8.	3 −2	9.	3 −3	10.	1 −1
11.	2 −2	12.	2 −1	13.	4 −1	14.	2 −2	15.	4 −3
16.	1 −0	17.	2 −0	18.	0 −0	19.	2 −0	20.	3 −0
21.	0 −0	22.	1 −1	23.	5 −4	24.	3 −1	25.	3 −1
26.	2 −1	27.	2 −1	28.	4 −0	29.	4 −4	30.	3 −0
31.	3 −0	32.	1 −0	33.	1 −1	34.	5 −1	35.	3 −0
36.	4 −0	37.	0 −0	38.	3 −0	39.	5 −4	40.	1 −0
41.	1 −0	42.	3 −1	43.	3 −1	44.	0 −0	45.	3 −1
46.	1 −1	47.	4 −4	48.	3 −1	49.	5 −3	50.	3 −1

SUBTRACTION
0 TO 5

Name: _____

Date: _____ Time: _____

Score:
___/50

1. 4
    -1
    _____

2. 5
    -2
    _____

3. 1
    -0
    _____

4. 0
    -0
    _____

5. 5
    -1
    _____

6. 1
    -1
    _____

7. 3
    -0
    _____

8. 2
    -2
    _____

9. 1
    -0
    _____

10. 2
    -1
    _____

11. 4
    -3
    _____

12. 0
    -0
    _____

13. 3
    -0
    _____

14. 4
    -0
    _____

15. 4
    -1
    _____

16. 0
    -0
    _____

17. 5
    -4
    _____

18. 2
    -1
    _____

19. 5
    -5
    _____

20. 1
    -0
    _____

21. 5
    -1
    _____

22. 4
    -3
    _____

23. 0
    -0
    _____

24. 4
    -4
    _____

25. 4
    -0
    _____

26. 4
    -4
    _____

27. 2
    -1
    _____

28. 2
    -1
    _____

29. 4
    -4
    _____

30. 3
    -0
    _____

31. 0
    -0
    _____

32. 3
    -1
    _____

33. 3
    -3
    _____

34. 0
    -0
    _____

35. 5
    -0
    _____

36. 4
    -2
    _____

37. 2
    -1
    _____

38. 1
    -0
    _____

39. 4
    -0
    _____

40. 3
    -1
    _____

41. 2
    -2
    _____

42. 3
    -2
    _____

43. 0
    -0
    _____

44. 5
    -2
    _____

45. 2
    -2
    _____

46. 0
    -0
    _____

47. 0
    -0
    _____

48. 4
    -1
    _____

49. 3
    -2
    _____

50. 3
    -1
    _____

prepaze

SUBTRACTION 0 TO 5

1. 5 -2	2. 2 -1	3. 1 -1	4. 2 -1	5. 4 -1
6. 0 -0	7. 1 -1	8. 3 -2	9. 2 -0	10. 4 -3
11. 3 -1	12. 5 -2	13. 0 -0	14. 5 -2	15. 4 -2
16. 2 -2	17. 4 -3	18. 2 -1	19. 2 -2	20. 4 -4
21. 4 -0	22. 3 -1	23. 3 -2	24. 0 -0	25. 4 -4
26. 2 -1	27. 1 -1	28. 1 -0	29. 0 -0	30. 0 -0
31. 3 -2	32. 4 -1	33. 4 -4	34. 5 -1	35. 1 -0
36. 0 -0	37. 1 -1	38. 4 -1	39. 5 -4	40. 2 -1
41. 4 -3	42. 2 -1	43. 1 -0	44. 4 -2	45. 0 -0
46. 1 -0	47. 0 -0	48. 3 -0	49. 2 -1	50. 1 -1

SUBTRACTION 0 TO 5

Name: _____

Date: _____ Time: _____

Score: /50

1. 0 -0	2. 1 -1	3. 1 -1	4. 3 -1	5. 4 -3

1.   0 − 0
2.   1 − 1
3.   1 − 1
4.   3 − 1
5.   4 − 3

6.   3 − 0
7.   4 − 3
8.   2 − 1
9.   4 − 2
10.   4 − 1

11.   1 − 1
12.   3 − 2
13.   2 − 0
14.   4 − 1
15.   2 − 0

16.   4 − 2
17.   3 − 3
18.   3 − 1
19.   2 − 1
20.   1 − 1

21.   3 − 2
22.   0 − 0
23.   3 − 1
24.   2 − 1
25.   0 − 0

26.   2 − 2
27.   0 − 0
28.   3 − 3
29.   1 − 1
30.   3 − 2

31.   3 − 3
32.   4 − 2
33.   5 − 5
34.   2 − 1
35.   1 − 0

36.   3 − 2
37.   2 − 1
38.   1 − 0
39.   0 − 0
40.   3 − 1

41.   4 − 0
42.   2 − 1
43.   5 − 4
44.   5 − 5
45.   2 − 0

46.   3 − 2
47.   2 − 1
48.   4 − 3
49.   2 − 2
50.   4 − 0

prepaze

SUBTRACTION
0 TO 5

Name: _____
Date: _____ Time: _____
Score: /50

1.   2
     -1
	2. 2
	     -2
		3. 2
		     -1
			4. 4
			     -3
				5. 1
				     -1

6.   3
     -1
	7. 4
	     -0
		8. 1
		     -0
			9. 0
			     -0
				10. 2
				     -1

11.   1
     -0
	12. 5
	     -4
		13. 1
		     -0
			14. 3
			     -1
				15. 5
				     -1

16.   5
     -4
	17. 1
	     -0
		18. 2
		     -1
			19. 5
			     -4
				20. 1
				     -1

21.   4
     -2
	22. 3
	     -1
		23. 1
		     -1
			24. 4
			     -3
				25. 3
				     -3

26.   2
     -2
	27. 0
	     -0
		28. 3
		     -1
			29. 4
			     -2
				30. 4
				     -0

31.   4
     -1
	32. 1
	     -1
		33. 0
		     -0
			34. 4
			     -1
				35. 3
				     -1

36.   1
     -0
	37. 2
	     -0
		38. 0
		     -0
			39. 1
			     -1
				40. 1
				     -0

41.   2
     -1
	42. 1
	     -0
		43. 2
		     -1
			44. 3
			     -0
				45. 5
				     -3

46.   2
     -2
	47. 3
	     -0
		48. 3
		     -1
			49. 0
			     -0
				50. 5
				     -0

SUBTRACTION 0 TO 5

1.	4 -1	2.	0 -0	3.	4 -2	4.	3 -1	5.	4 -1
6.	0 -0	7.	0 -0	8.	2 -0	9.	3 -0	10.	2 -0
11.	3 -1	12.	4 -1	13.	2 -1	14.	3 -2	15.	0 -0
16.	2 -1	17.	0 -0	18.	1 -0	19.	4 -3	20.	1 -1
21.	2 -0	22.	4 -2	23.	1 -0	24.	2 -1	25.	0 -0
26.	1 -1	27.	3 -1	28.	2 -1	29.	3 -1	30.	5 -5
31.	1 -1	32.	1 -1	33.	4 -3	34.	4 -0	35.	4 -1
36.	0 -0	37.	2 -1	38.	4 -1	39.	0 -0	40.	1 -1
41.	3 -2	42.	0 -0	43.	3 -1	44.	1 -1	45.	0 -0
46.	3 -1	47.	0 -0	48.	0 -0	49.	4 -4	50.	4 -0

SUBTRACTION 0 TO 5

Name: _____

Date: _____ Time: _____

Score: __/50

1. 1 −1	2. 1 −1	3. 3 −3	4. 5 −0	5. 3 −0
6. 4 −1	7. 4 −1	8. 5 −2	9. 3 −3	10. 2 −2
11. 4 −3	12. 3 −3	13. 3 −1	14. 5 −1	15. 2 −1
16. 3 −2	17. 0 −0	18. 3 −2	19. 4 −0	20. 2 −1
21. 3 −2	22. 3 −2	23. 1 −1	24. 3 −2	25. 3 −1
26. 2 −2	27. 5 −5	28. 1 −0	29. 3 −2	30. 0 −0
31. 4 −3	32. 3 −1	33. 0 −0	34. 3 −2	35. 2 −0
36. 1 −0	37. 1 −1	38. 3 −0	39. 4 −0	40. 2 −0
41. 5 −4	42. 4 −2	43. 4 −3	44. 2 −1	45. 5 −4
46. 0 −0	47. 0 −0	48. 2 −1	49. 3 −3	50. 4 −2

prepaze

www.prepaze.com

Name: _____

Date: _____ Time: _____

1.   2
    -0
	2. 3
	    -1
		3. 1
		    -1
			4. 1
			    -1
				5. 0
				    -0

6.   3
    -2
	7. 5
	    -1
		8. 5
		    -5
			9. 5
			    -0
				10. 1
				    -0

11.   1
    -0
	12. 1
	    -0
		13. 4
		    -3
			14. 1
			    -1
				15. 2
				    -2

16.   0
    -0
	17. 5
	    -1
		18. 3
		    -2
			19. 1
			    -0
				20. 2
				    -1

21.   0
    -0
	22. 2
	    -1
		23. 0
		    -0
			24. 3
			    -1
				25. 0
				    -0

26.   5
    -5
	27. 3
	    -2
		28. 0
		    -0
			29. 4
			    -2
				30. 4
				    -0

31.   0
    -0
	32. 3
	    -1
		33. 5
		    -2
			34. 4
			    -0
				35. 0
				    -0

36.   1
    -0
	37. 4
	    -3
		38. 4
		    -1
			39. 1
			    -0
				40. 2
				    -1

41.   3
    -2
	42. 1
	    -0
		43. 2
		    -0
			44. 2
			    -1
				45. 3
				    -1

46.   4
    -3
	47. 3
	    -3
		48. 0
		    -0
			49. 5
			    -2
				50. 0
				    -0

SUBTRACT THE NUMBERS

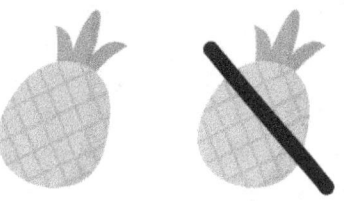

  $2 - 1 =$

 $3 - 2 =$

   $4 - 2 =$

   $3 - 3 =$

     $5 - 4 =$

WORD PROBLEMS
SUBTRACTION 0 TO 5

Name: _____
Date: _____ Time: _____

1. Greg had 5 crayons . He gave 2 crayons to Charlie. How many crayons does Greg have left?

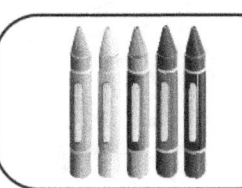

ANSWER

2. There were 4 turtles near the shore. 3 of them swam away. How many turtles are left near the shore?

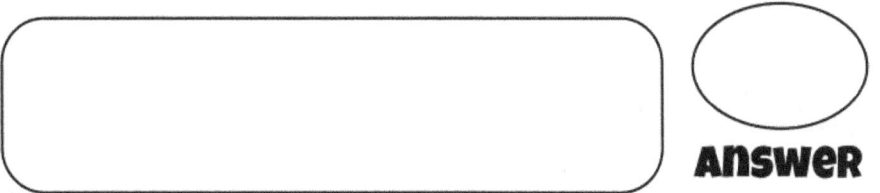

ANSWER

3. There were 2 caterpillars in the garden. 1 of them crawled away. How many caterpillars are left in the garden?

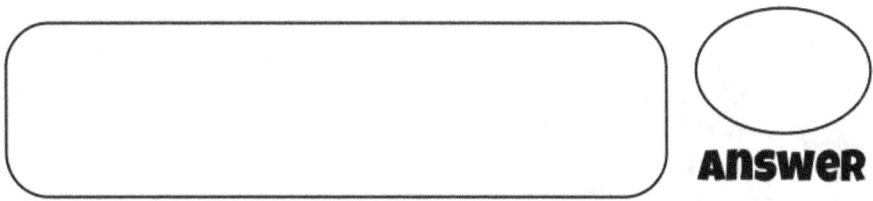

ANSWER

4. There were 4 melons in the garden. 2 of them were harvested. How many melons are left in the garden?

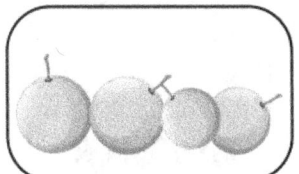

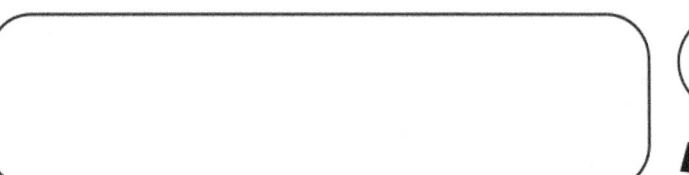

ANSWER

prepaze

5. Katie had 3 marbles. She gave 3 of them to John. How many marbles does Annie have left?

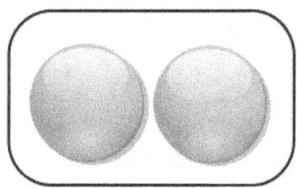

ANSWER

6. James had 2 oranges. He gave 1 of them to Lucy. How many apples does James have left?

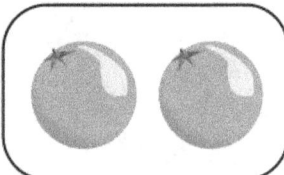

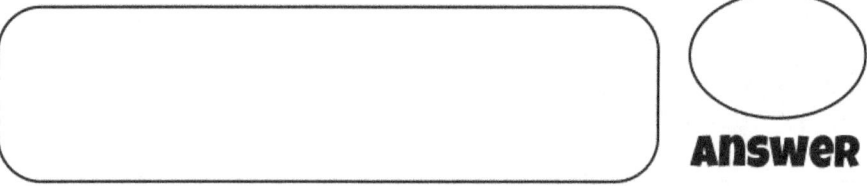

ANSWER

7. Ruby had 4 apples. She gave 2 of them to Trent. How many apples does Ruby have left?

ANSWER

8. There were 3 chicks. 1 of them ran away. How many chicks are left?

ANSWER

9. Luke had 4 ribbons. He gave 4 of them to Blake. How many ribbons does Luke have left?

ANSWER

10. Dan caught 2 bluefish in the lake. 1 of them swam away. How many bluefish does Dan have now?

ANSWER

11. There are 5 sandcastles on the shore. 2 are washed away how many are left now?

 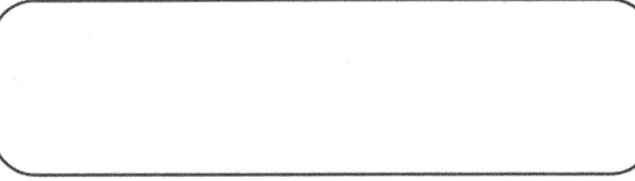 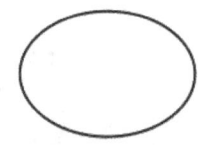

ANSWER

12. Shery has $5. She buys a candy for $2. How much does she have now?

 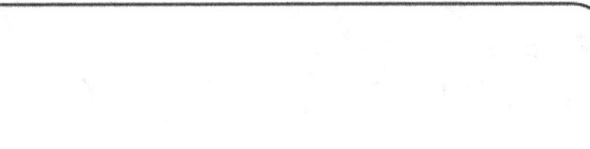 

ANSWER

SUBTRACT THE NUMBERS

13. There are 4 dragonflies. If 3 flew away, how many dragonflies are there now?

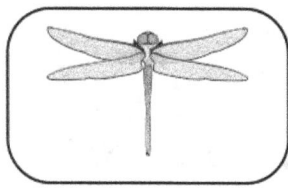  

ANSWER

14. Ryan has 5 toy cars. He gave 2 toy cars to his friend. How many toy cars does Ryan have now?

 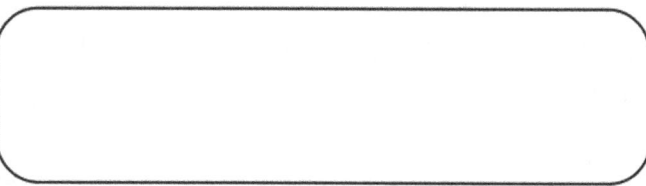

ANSWER

15. Sia has 2 chocolates. She gave 2 chocolates to her friends. How many chocolates does Sia have now?

 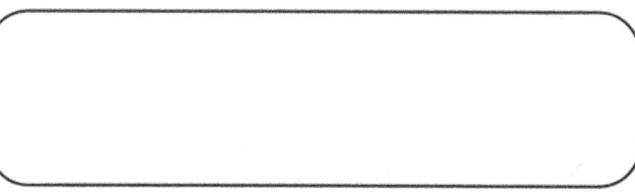 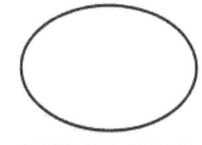

ANSWER

16. Aunt Sally bought 5 balloons. She kept 2 balloons with her and gave the rest of the balloons to her niece. How many balloons did she give to her niece?

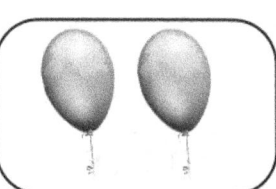  

ANSWER

WORD PROBLEMS
SUBTRACTION 0 TO 5

Name: _____
Date: _____ Time: _____

17. There were 3 pears in a basket. Charles ate 1 pear. How many pears are left over?

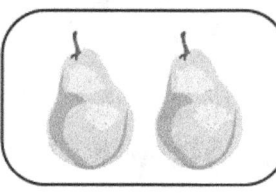

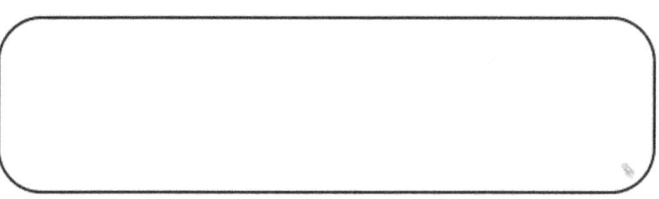

ANSWER

18. Laurie has 3 crayons. On coloring, 1 crayon broke. How many unbroken crayons does he have now?

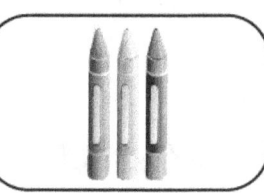

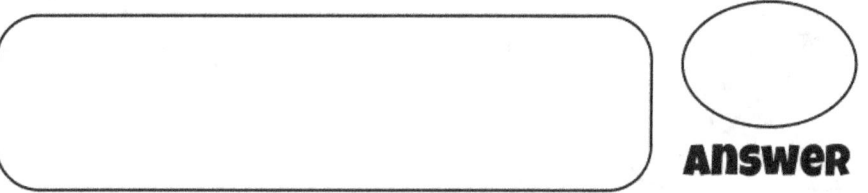

ANSWER

19. Jack needs 5 flowers to make a bouquet. He collected 3 flowers. How many more flowers does he need to make the bouquets?

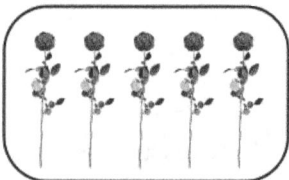

ANSWER

20. Harry had 3 gumballs. He gave 1 to his sister. How gumballs does he have now?

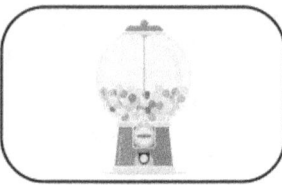

ANSWER

WORD PROBLEMS
SUBTRACTION 0 TO 5

Name: _____
Date: _____ Time: _____

21. Kelly made 3 cupcakes for the carnival. 2 were vanilla flavoured and the rest were chocolate flavoured. How many cupcakes were chocolate flavoured?

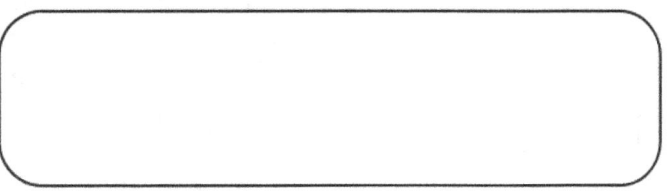

ANSWER

22. Liu colored 2 flowers. Barry colored 3 flowers. How many more flowers did Barry color than Liu?

ANSWER

23. There are 5 balls in the basket. 1 of them is red in color while others are blue in color. How many balls are blue in color?

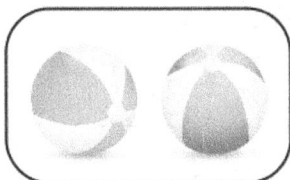

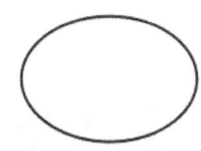

ANSWER

24. Jenny has $3. She saves $2 and spends the rest. How much does she have now?

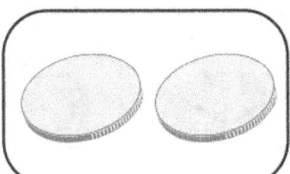

ANSWER

WORD PROBLEMS
SUBTRACTION 0 TO 5

Name: ______________________
Date: __________ Time: __________

25. Shelly collected 5 shells. She gave 1 shell to her brother. How many shells does she have now?

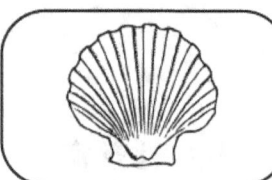

Answer

ACTIVITY CORNER

COLORING ACTIVITY

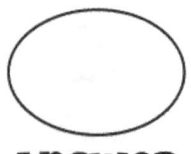

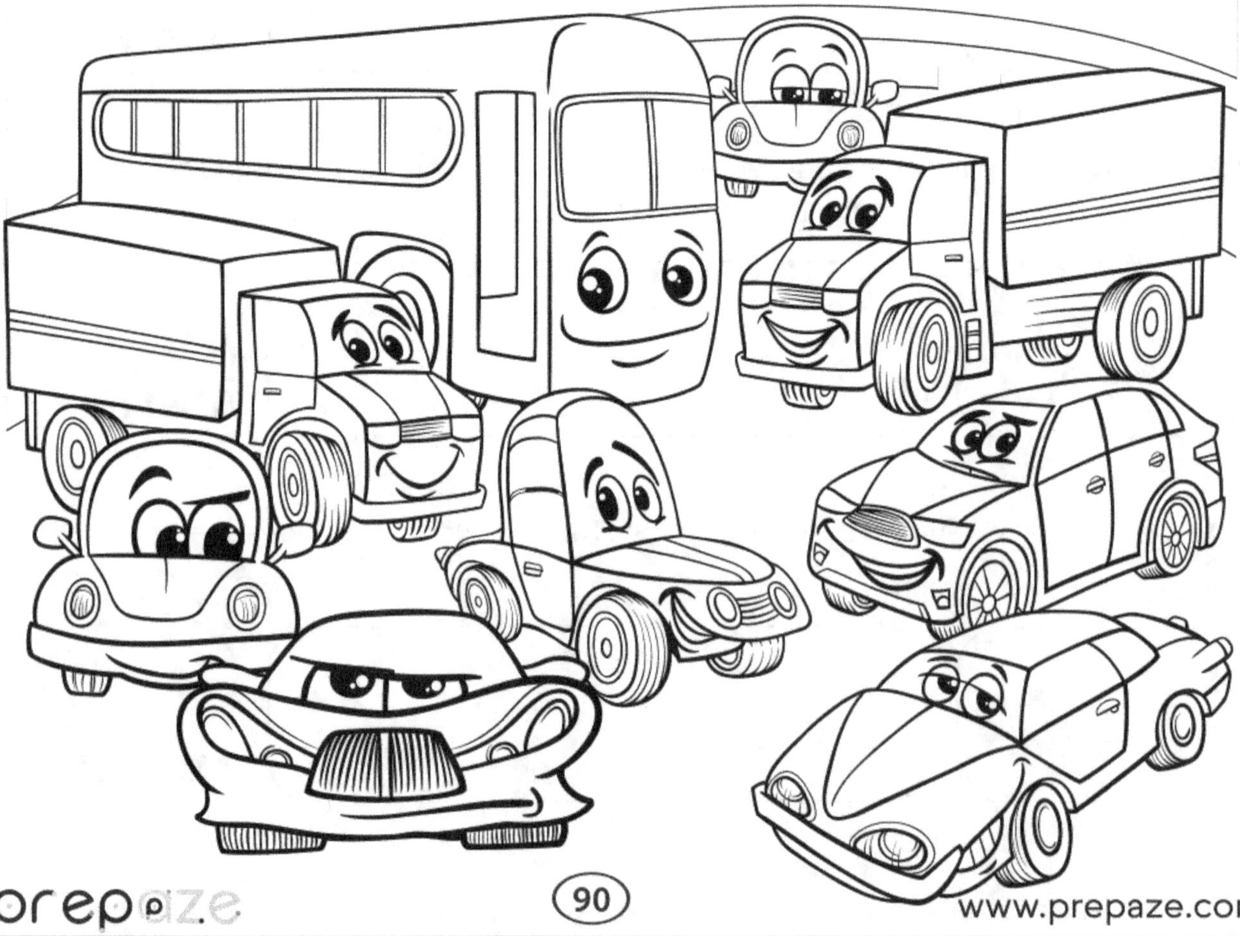

1. $\begin{array}{r} 7 \\ -6 \\ \hline \end{array}$	2. $\begin{array}{r} 7 \\ -7 \\ \hline \end{array}$	3. $\begin{array}{r} 7 \\ -7 \\ \hline \end{array}$	4. $\begin{array}{r} 10 \\ -9 \\ \hline \end{array}$	5. $\begin{array}{r} 9 \\ -6 \\ \hline \end{array}$
6. $\begin{array}{r} 6 \\ -6 \\ \hline \end{array}$	7. $\begin{array}{r} 9 \\ -7 \\ \hline \end{array}$	8. $\begin{array}{r} 6 \\ -6 \\ \hline \end{array}$	9. $\begin{array}{r} 9 \\ -8 \\ \hline \end{array}$	10. $\begin{array}{r} 7 \\ -7 \\ \hline \end{array}$
11. $\begin{array}{r} 6 \\ -6 \\ \hline \end{array}$	12. $\begin{array}{r} 10 \\ -8 \\ \hline \end{array}$	13. $\begin{array}{r} 8 \\ -8 \\ \hline \end{array}$	14. $\begin{array}{r} 9 \\ -7 \\ \hline \end{array}$	15. $\begin{array}{r} 10 \\ -6 \\ \hline \end{array}$
16. $\begin{array}{r} 8 \\ -6 \\ \hline \end{array}$	17. $\begin{array}{r} 10 \\ -10 \\ \hline \end{array}$	18. $\begin{array}{r} 7 \\ -7 \\ \hline \end{array}$	19. $\begin{array}{r} 9 \\ -8 \\ \hline \end{array}$	20. $\begin{array}{r} 9 \\ -8 \\ \hline \end{array}$
21. $\begin{array}{r} 6 \\ -6 \\ \hline \end{array}$	22. $\begin{array}{r} 10 \\ -7 \\ \hline \end{array}$	23. $\begin{array}{r} 7 \\ -6 \\ \hline \end{array}$	24. $\begin{array}{r} 8 \\ -6 \\ \hline \end{array}$	25. $\begin{array}{r} 10 \\ -9 \\ \hline \end{array}$
26. $\begin{array}{r} 6 \\ -6 \\ \hline \end{array}$	27. $\begin{array}{r} 10 \\ -7 \\ \hline \end{array}$	28. $\begin{array}{r} 6 \\ -6 \\ \hline \end{array}$	29. $\begin{array}{r} 6 \\ -6 \\ \hline \end{array}$	30. $\begin{array}{r} 8 \\ -7 \\ \hline \end{array}$
31. $\begin{array}{r} 9 \\ -9 \\ \hline \end{array}$	32. $\begin{array}{r} 8 \\ -8 \\ \hline \end{array}$	33. $\begin{array}{r} 6 \\ -6 \\ \hline \end{array}$	34. $\begin{array}{r} 8 \\ -6 \\ \hline \end{array}$	35. $\begin{array}{r} 8 \\ -7 \\ \hline \end{array}$
36. $\begin{array}{r} 8 \\ -6 \\ \hline \end{array}$	37. $\begin{array}{r} 10 \\ -8 \\ \hline \end{array}$	38. $\begin{array}{r} 8 \\ -7 \\ \hline \end{array}$	39. $\begin{array}{r} 9 \\ -6 \\ \hline \end{array}$	40. $\begin{array}{r} 10 \\ -8 \\ \hline \end{array}$
41. $\begin{array}{r} 10 \\ -8 \\ \hline \end{array}$	42. $\begin{array}{r} 7 \\ -7 \\ \hline \end{array}$	43. $\begin{array}{r} 6 \\ -6 \\ \hline \end{array}$	44. $\begin{array}{r} 7 \\ -6 \\ \hline \end{array}$	45. $\begin{array}{r} 10 \\ -9 \\ \hline \end{array}$
46. $\begin{array}{r} 6 \\ -6 \\ \hline \end{array}$	47. $\begin{array}{r} 10 \\ -9 \\ \hline \end{array}$	48. $\begin{array}{r} 10 \\ -6 \\ \hline \end{array}$	49. $\begin{array}{r} 7 \\ -6 \\ \hline \end{array}$	50. $\begin{array}{r} 9 \\ -6 \\ \hline \end{array}$

SUBTRACTION 6 TO 10

Name: _____

Date: _____ Time: _____

Score: /50

1.	9 -7	2.	9 -7	3.	9 -8	4.	10 -8	5.	10 -8
6.	10 -10	7.	7 -6	8.	9 -7	9.	8 -7	10.	8 -6
11.	9 -8	12.	6 -6	13.	10 -6	14.	7 -6	15.	7 -6
16.	7 -6	17.	9 -7	18.	7 -7	19.	7 -7	20.	8 -8
21.	7 -6	22.	7 -6	23.	6 -6	24.	8 -7	25.	7 -7
26.	7 -7	27.	8 -8	28.	7 -6	29.	7 -7	30.	8 -8
31.	10 -8	32.	9 -9	33.	7 -7	34.	6 -6	35.	9 -8
36.	8 -6	37.	7 -6	38.	6 -6	39.	7 -6	40.	10 -10
41.	8 -7	42.	8 -6	43.	7 -7	44.	10 -8	45.	9 -8
46.	10 -9	47.	7 -7	48.	7 -6	49.	9 -7	50.	10 -7

prepaze

www.prepaze.com

SUBTRACTION 6 TO 10

1. $\begin{array}{r} 9 \\ -8 \\ \hline \end{array}$	2. $\begin{array}{r} 6 \\ -6 \\ \hline \end{array}$	3. $\begin{array}{r} 8 \\ -7 \\ \hline \end{array}$	4. $\begin{array}{r} 7 \\ -6 \\ \hline \end{array}$	5. $\begin{array}{r} 8 \\ -7 \\ \hline \end{array}$
6. $\begin{array}{r} 9 \\ -8 \\ \hline \end{array}$	7. $\begin{array}{r} 7 \\ -6 \\ \hline \end{array}$	8. $\begin{array}{r} 8 \\ -8 \\ \hline \end{array}$	9. $\begin{array}{r} 9 \\ -8 \\ \hline \end{array}$	10. $\begin{array}{r} 6 \\ -6 \\ \hline \end{array}$
11. $\begin{array}{r} 6 \\ -6 \\ \hline \end{array}$	12. $\begin{array}{r} 9 \\ -6 \\ \hline \end{array}$	13. $\begin{array}{r} 6 \\ -6 \\ \hline \end{array}$	14. $\begin{array}{r} 8 \\ -8 \\ \hline \end{array}$	15. $\begin{array}{r} 7 \\ -6 \\ \hline \end{array}$
16. $\begin{array}{r} 10 \\ -9 \\ \hline \end{array}$	17. $\begin{array}{r} 6 \\ -6 \\ \hline \end{array}$	18. $\begin{array}{r} 8 \\ -8 \\ \hline \end{array}$	19. $\begin{array}{r} 8 \\ -8 \\ \hline \end{array}$	20. $\begin{array}{r} 10 \\ -8 \\ \hline \end{array}$
21. $\begin{array}{r} 6 \\ -6 \\ \hline \end{array}$	22. $\begin{array}{r} 7 \\ -7 \\ \hline \end{array}$	23. $\begin{array}{r} 8 \\ -8 \\ \hline \end{array}$	24. $\begin{array}{r} 9 \\ -8 \\ \hline \end{array}$	25. $\begin{array}{r} 7 \\ -7 \\ \hline \end{array}$
26. $\begin{array}{r} 10 \\ -6 \\ \hline \end{array}$	27. $\begin{array}{r} 9 \\ -9 \\ \hline \end{array}$	28. $\begin{array}{r} 7 \\ -6 \\ \hline \end{array}$	29. $\begin{array}{r} 7 \\ -6 \\ \hline \end{array}$	30. $\begin{array}{r} 8 \\ -7 \\ \hline \end{array}$
31. $\begin{array}{r} 6 \\ -6 \\ \hline \end{array}$	32. $\begin{array}{r} 7 \\ -6 \\ \hline \end{array}$	33. $\begin{array}{r} 7 \\ -6 \\ \hline \end{array}$	34. $\begin{array}{r} 8 \\ -7 \\ \hline \end{array}$	35. $\begin{array}{r} 8 \\ -7 \\ \hline \end{array}$
36. $\begin{array}{r} 8 \\ -8 \\ \hline \end{array}$	37. $\begin{array}{r} 9 \\ -6 \\ \hline \end{array}$	38. $\begin{array}{r} 7 \\ -7 \\ \hline \end{array}$	39. $\begin{array}{r} 8 \\ -7 \\ \hline \end{array}$	40. $\begin{array}{r} 6 \\ -6 \\ \hline \end{array}$
41. $\begin{array}{r} 8 \\ -8 \\ \hline \end{array}$	42. $\begin{array}{r} 10 \\ -8 \\ \hline \end{array}$	43. $\begin{array}{r} 10 \\ -7 \\ \hline \end{array}$	44. $\begin{array}{r} 6 \\ -6 \\ \hline \end{array}$	45. $\begin{array}{r} 8 \\ -6 \\ \hline \end{array}$
46. $\begin{array}{r} 8 \\ -7 \\ \hline \end{array}$	47. $\begin{array}{r} 8 \\ -6 \\ \hline \end{array}$	48. $\begin{array}{r} 7 \\ -7 \\ \hline \end{array}$	49. $\begin{array}{r} 8 \\ -6 \\ \hline \end{array}$	50. $\begin{array}{r} 7 \\ -6 \\ \hline \end{array}$

prepaze

SUBTRACTION 6 TO 10

Name: _____

Date: _____ Time: _____

Score: /50

1. $\begin{array}{r} 7 \\ -7 \\ \hline \end{array}$
2. $\begin{array}{r} 7 \\ -6 \\ \hline \end{array}$
3. $\begin{array}{r} 9 \\ -7 \\ \hline \end{array}$
4. $\begin{array}{r} 10 \\ -7 \\ \hline \end{array}$
5. $\begin{array}{r} 9 \\ -8 \\ \hline \end{array}$

6. $\begin{array}{r} 8 \\ -8 \\ \hline \end{array}$
7. $\begin{array}{r} 9 \\ -7 \\ \hline \end{array}$
8. $\begin{array}{r} 6 \\ -6 \\ \hline \end{array}$
9. $\begin{array}{r} 8 \\ -7 \\ \hline \end{array}$
10. $\begin{array}{r} 9 \\ -8 \\ \hline \end{array}$

11. $\begin{array}{r} 7 \\ -7 \\ \hline \end{array}$
12. $\begin{array}{r} 7 \\ -6 \\ \hline \end{array}$
13. $\begin{array}{r} 6 \\ -6 \\ \hline \end{array}$
14. $\begin{array}{r} 6 \\ -6 \\ \hline \end{array}$
15. $\begin{array}{r} 6 \\ -6 \\ \hline \end{array}$

16. $\begin{array}{r} 7 \\ -6 \\ \hline \end{array}$
17. $\begin{array}{r} 7 \\ -7 \\ \hline \end{array}$
18. $\begin{array}{r} 8 \\ -6 \\ \hline \end{array}$
19. $\begin{array}{r} 9 \\ -9 \\ \hline \end{array}$
20. $\begin{array}{r} 8 \\ -7 \\ \hline \end{array}$

21. $\begin{array}{r} 6 \\ -6 \\ \hline \end{array}$
22. $\begin{array}{r} 9 \\ -8 \\ \hline \end{array}$
23. $\begin{array}{r} 6 \\ -6 \\ \hline \end{array}$
24. $\begin{array}{r} 10 \\ -8 \\ \hline \end{array}$
25. $\begin{array}{r} 10 \\ -8 \\ \hline \end{array}$

26. $\begin{array}{r} 7 \\ -6 \\ \hline \end{array}$
27. $\begin{array}{r} 8 \\ -7 \\ \hline \end{array}$
28. $\begin{array}{r} 10 \\ -8 \\ \hline \end{array}$
29. $\begin{array}{r} 6 \\ -6 \\ \hline \end{array}$
30. $\begin{array}{r} 7 \\ -6 \\ \hline \end{array}$

31. $\begin{array}{r} 9 \\ -7 \\ \hline \end{array}$
32. $\begin{array}{r} 9 \\ -8 \\ \hline \end{array}$
33. $\begin{array}{r} 9 \\ -7 \\ \hline \end{array}$
34. $\begin{array}{r} 9 \\ -6 \\ \hline \end{array}$
35. $\begin{array}{r} 9 \\ -7 \\ \hline \end{array}$

36. $\begin{array}{r} 9 \\ -9 \\ \hline \end{array}$
37. $\begin{array}{r} 10 \\ -7 \\ \hline \end{array}$
38. $\begin{array}{r} 7 \\ -6 \\ \hline \end{array}$
39. $\begin{array}{r} 7 \\ -6 \\ \hline \end{array}$
40. $\begin{array}{r} 7 \\ -6 \\ \hline \end{array}$

41. $\begin{array}{r} 9 \\ -8 \\ \hline \end{array}$
42. $\begin{array}{r} 9 \\ -8 \\ \hline \end{array}$
43. $\begin{array}{r} 8 \\ -7 \\ \hline \end{array}$
44. $\begin{array}{r} 6 \\ -6 \\ \hline \end{array}$
45. $\begin{array}{r} 7 \\ -7 \\ \hline \end{array}$

46. $\begin{array}{r} 8 \\ -7 \\ \hline \end{array}$
47. $\begin{array}{r} 6 \\ -6 \\ \hline \end{array}$
48. $\begin{array}{r} 6 \\ -6 \\ \hline \end{array}$
49. $\begin{array}{r} 8 \\ -7 \\ \hline \end{array}$
50. $\begin{array}{r} 7 \\ -6 \\ \hline \end{array}$

1.   9
    -8
	2. 9
	    -8
		3. 8
		    -7

1.   9
   -8

2.   9
   -8

3.   8
   -7

4.   10
   -7

5.   7
   -6

6.   8
   -8

7.   8
   -6

8.   9
   -8

9.   8
   -8

10.   8
   -6

11.   9
   -8

12.   8
   -7

13.   10
   -7

14.   9
   -7

15.   8
   -7

16.   9
   -7

17.   10
   -8

18.   9
   -7

19.   7
   -7

20.   7
   -7

21.   9
   -7

22.   9
   -6

23.   7
   -7

24.   8
   -7

25.   6
   -6

26.   9
   -8

27.   9
   -9

28.   10
   -9

29.   10
   -10

30.   8
   -7

31.   8
   -8

32.   8
   -7

33.   9
   -9

34.   7
   -7

35.   9
   -9

36.   8
   -6

37.   7
   -6

38.   7
   -6

39.   9
   -8

40.   9
   -8

41.   10
   -6

42.   8
   -8

43.   8
   -8

44.   7
   -7

45.   9
   -6

46.   7
   -6

47.   6
   -6

48.   8
   -8

49.   8
   -7

50.   10
   -6

prepaze

1.	8 −7	2.	6 −6	3.	9 −9	4.	8 −7	5.	7 −7
6.	8 −8	7.	9 −6	8.	8 −7	9.	7 −6	10.	9 −8
11.	6 −6	12.	8 −7	13.	7 −6	14.	6 −6	15.	10 −9
16.	9 −7	17.	9 −9	18.	8 −8	19.	6 −6	20.	7 −6
21.	8 −6	22.	7 −7	23.	10 −10	24.	9 −7	25.	9 −9
26.	6 −6	27.	8 −6	28.	9 −9	29.	9 −7	30.	8 −6
31.	8 −7	32.	6 −6	33.	7 −7	34.	8 −7	35.	7 −6
36.	7 −7	37.	6 −6	38.	7 −7	39.	9 −9	40.	8 −7
41.	6 −6	42.	9 −8	43.	9 −7	44.	9 −9	45.	9 −9
46.	7 −7	47.	9 −9	48.	6 −6	49.	6 −6	50.	7 −7

1. $\begin{array}{r} 10 \\ -7 \\ \hline \end{array}$	2. $\begin{array}{r} 6 \\ -6 \\ \hline \end{array}$	3. $\begin{array}{r} 8 \\ -7 \\ \hline \end{array}$	4. $\begin{array}{r} 6 \\ -6 \\ \hline \end{array}$	5. $\begin{array}{r} 9 \\ -7 \\ \hline \end{array}$
6. $\begin{array}{r} 10 \\ -7 \\ \hline \end{array}$	7. $\begin{array}{r} 7 \\ -7 \\ \hline \end{array}$	8. $\begin{array}{r} 9 \\ -7 \\ \hline \end{array}$	9. $\begin{array}{r} 9 \\ -8 \\ \hline \end{array}$	10. $\begin{array}{r} 8 \\ -7 \\ \hline \end{array}$
11. $\begin{array}{r} 6 \\ -6 \\ \hline \end{array}$	12. $\begin{array}{r} 8 \\ -6 \\ \hline \end{array}$	13. $\begin{array}{r} 8 \\ -6 \\ \hline \end{array}$	14. $\begin{array}{r} 9 \\ -8 \\ \hline \end{array}$	15. $\begin{array}{r} 9 \\ -9 \\ \hline \end{array}$
16. $\begin{array}{r} 9 \\ -9 \\ \hline \end{array}$	17. $\begin{array}{r} 8 \\ -6 \\ \hline \end{array}$	18. $\begin{array}{r} 9 \\ -8 \\ \hline \end{array}$	19. $\begin{array}{r} 6 \\ -6 \\ \hline \end{array}$	20. $\begin{array}{r} 9 \\ -7 \\ \hline \end{array}$
21. $\begin{array}{r} 6 \\ -6 \\ \hline \end{array}$	22. $\begin{array}{r} 8 \\ -6 \\ \hline \end{array}$	23. $\begin{array}{r} 6 \\ -6 \\ \hline \end{array}$	24. $\begin{array}{r} 8 \\ -7 \\ \hline \end{array}$	25. $\begin{array}{r} 7 \\ -7 \\ \hline \end{array}$
26. $\begin{array}{r} 8 \\ -7 \\ \hline \end{array}$	27. $\begin{array}{r} 6 \\ -6 \\ \hline \end{array}$	28. $\begin{array}{r} 7 \\ -7 \\ \hline \end{array}$	29. $\begin{array}{r} 6 \\ -6 \\ \hline \end{array}$	30. $\begin{array}{r} 8 \\ -7 \\ \hline \end{array}$
31. $\begin{array}{r} 6 \\ -6 \\ \hline \end{array}$	32. $\begin{array}{r} 8 \\ -6 \\ \hline \end{array}$	33. $\begin{array}{r} 8 \\ -7 \\ \hline \end{array}$	34. $\begin{array}{r} 9 \\ -9 \\ \hline \end{array}$	35. $\begin{array}{r} 9 \\ -7 \\ \hline \end{array}$
36. $\begin{array}{r} 8 \\ -6 \\ \hline \end{array}$	37. $\begin{array}{r} 9 \\ -9 \\ \hline \end{array}$	38. $\begin{array}{r} 9 \\ -7 \\ \hline \end{array}$	39. $\begin{array}{r} 9 \\ -9 \\ \hline \end{array}$	40. $\begin{array}{r} 9 \\ -7 \\ \hline \end{array}$
41. $\begin{array}{r} 9 \\ -7 \\ \hline \end{array}$	42. $\begin{array}{r} 10 \\ -9 \\ \hline \end{array}$	43. $\begin{array}{r} 7 \\ -7 \\ \hline \end{array}$	44. $\begin{array}{r} 6 \\ -6 \\ \hline \end{array}$	45. $\begin{array}{r} 8 \\ -7 \\ \hline \end{array}$
46. $\begin{array}{r} 7 \\ -6 \\ \hline \end{array}$	47. $\begin{array}{r} 10 \\ -9 \\ \hline \end{array}$	48. $\begin{array}{r} 10 \\ -9 \\ \hline \end{array}$	49. $\begin{array}{r} 8 \\ -7 \\ \hline \end{array}$	50. $\begin{array}{r} 10 \\ -10 \\ \hline \end{array}$

prepaze

SUBTRACTION 6 TO 10

Name: _____

Date: _____ Time: _____

1.	10 -7	2.	10 -6	3.	8 -7	4.	8 -6	5.	9 -6
6.	10 -9	7.	8 -7	8.	10 -10	9.	9 -7	10.	7 -6
11.	8 -7	12.	9 -7	13.	7 -6	14.	8 -7	15.	9 -8
16.	7 -6	17.	7 -7	18.	6 -6	19.	7 -6	20.	7 -6
21.	10 -7	22.	8 -6	23.	7 -6	24.	10 -7	25.	10 -7
26.	7 -6	27.	8 -7	28.	8 -6	29.	9 -6	30.	7 -7
31.	6 -6	32.	10 -6	33.	6 -6	34.	9 -9	35.	8 -8
36.	8 -8	37.	6 -6	38.	9 -9	39.	8 -7	40.	8 -7
41.	6 -6	42.	9 -9	43.	6 -6	44.	7 -6	45.	6 -6
46.	10 -6	47.	9 -8	48.	9 -6	49.	10 -9	50.	8 -6

SUBTRACT THE NUMBERS

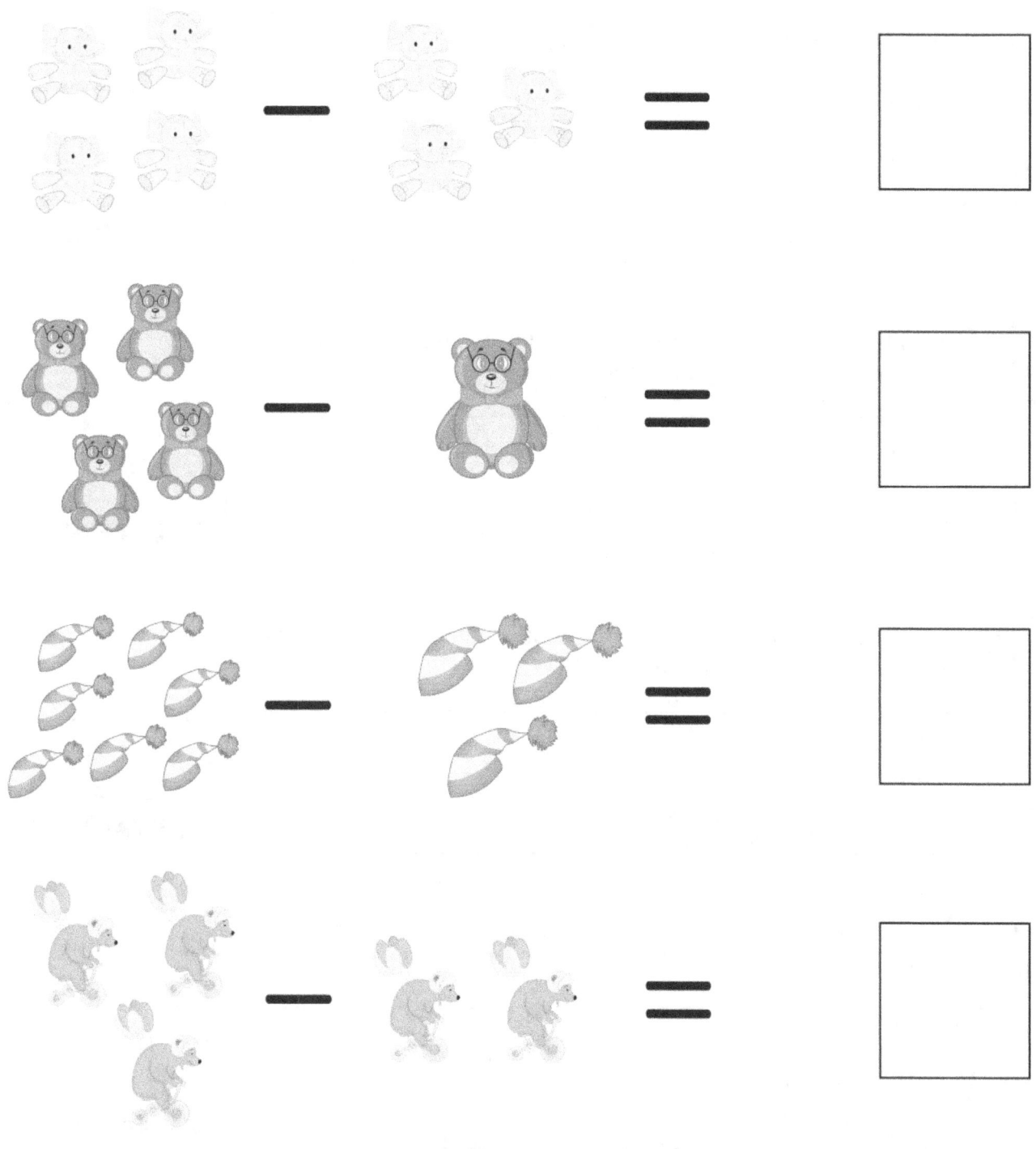

WORD PROBLEMS
SUBTRACTION 6 TO 10

1. I see 10 birds. 6 flew away. How many are left?

answer

2. Merlin had 8 balloons. Her friend Dan popped 6 balloons. How many balloons Merlin has now?

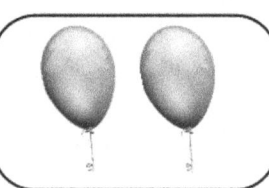  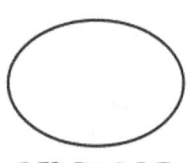

answer

3. Jack fetched up 9 buckets of water. Jill spilled down 8 buckets of water. How many buckets of water are left?

 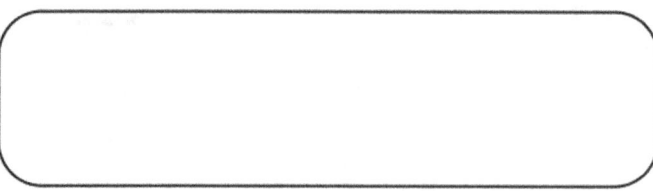 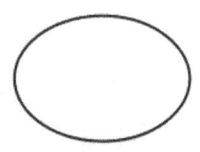

answer

4. The aquarium had 10 fish. Jan removed 6 fish. How many fish are left in the aquarium?

answer

WORD PROBLEMS
SUBTRACTION 6 TO 10

Name: _____
Date: _____ Time: _____

5. Daniel had 7 cookies. He gave away 6 of them to his friend. How many cookies does Daniel have left?

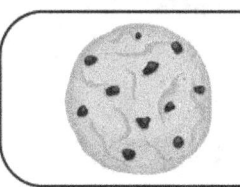

ANSWER

6. Martin collected 6 stickers. He lost 6 stickers. How many stickers is he left with now?

ANSWER

7. Ten gifts were there in the basket. Six are red and the rest are green. How many gifts are green?

ANSWER

8. Megan had 6 seashells. How many more does she need to have to make a 9?

ANSWER

WORD PROBLEMS
SUBTRACTION 6 TO 10

Name: _____
Date: _____ Time: _____

9. Joseph made 9 black kites. He gave 7 of them to his friend. How many kites does he have now?

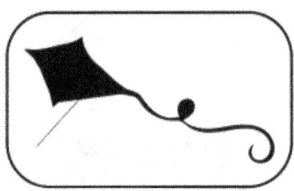

 **ANSWER**

10. There are 10 cars in a parking lot. 3 cars left. How many cars left in the parking lot now?

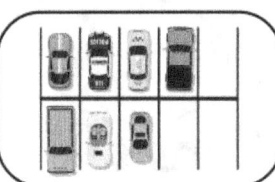

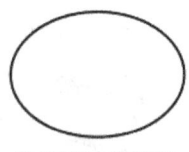 **ANSWER**

11. Tony had 8 pens he gave 6 pens to his friends. How many pens does he have now?

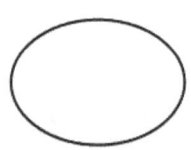 **ANSWER**

12. There are 10 sharpeners. 8 sharpeners are blue in color and the rest are red. How many erasers are red?

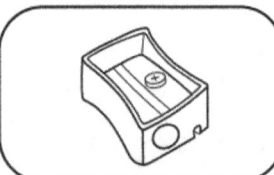

 **ANSWER**

FIND THE 10 DIFFERENCES

prepaze

WORD PROBLEMS
SUBTRACTION 6 TO 10

Name: _____
Date: _____ Time: _____

13. There are 9 robins and 8 bluejays in the tree. How many more robins are there than bluejays?

ANSWER

14. Beth has 8 action figures and Eva has 10 action figures. How many more action figures does Beth have than Eva?

ANSWER

15. James has 6 crayons and Scott has 7 crayons. How many more crayons does James have than Scott?

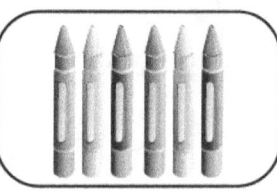

ANSWER

16. Tate has 8 pencils and Andy has 7 pencils. How many more pencils does Tate have than Andy?

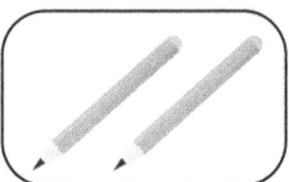

ANSWER

WORD PROBLEMS
SUBTRACTION 6 TO 10

Name: _____
Date: _____ Time: _____

17. Andrew has 10 flowers and Jess has 7 flowers. How many more flowers does Andrew have than Jess?

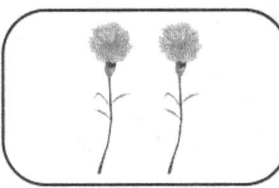  

ANSWER

18. There are 8 sunfish and 6 bluefish in the lake. How many more sunfish are there than bluefish?

ANSWER

19. There are 10 carrots and 8 cabbages in the garden. How many more carrots are there than cabbages ?

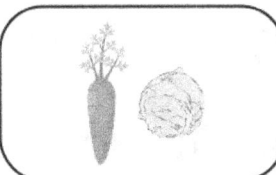 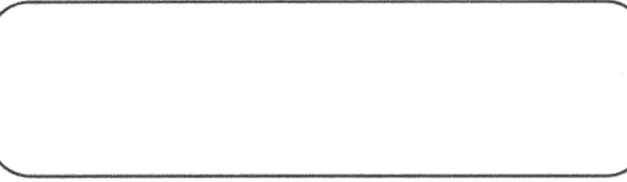 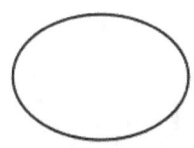

ANSWER

20. Bo built 10 snowmans and Zane built 6 snowmans. How many more snowmans did Bo build than Zane?

ANSWER

prepaze

WORD PROBLEMS
SUBTRACTION 6 TO 10

Name: _____
Date: _____ Time: _____

21. Wade has 7 pumpkins and Beth has 6 pumpkins . How many more pumpkins does Wade have than Beth?

 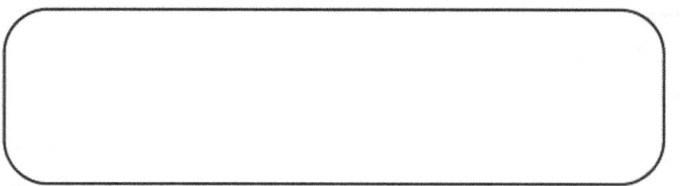 **ANSWER**

22. There are 9 bluefish and 7 salmon in the pond. How many more bluefish are there than salmon?

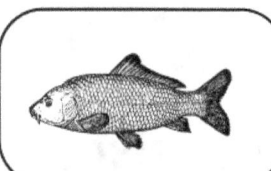  **ANSWER**

23. David had 9 marbles and he gave 6 marbles to his friend. How many marbles does he have?

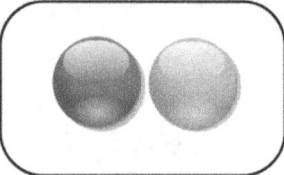  **ANSWER**

24. Jack says 8 taken away from 10 is 2. Is he right?

 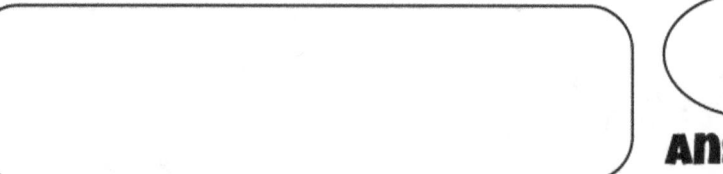  **ANSWER**

WORD PROBLEMS
SUBTRACTION 6 TO 10

25. A farmer has 10 pigs and 6 cows. How many more pigs does he have than cows?

ANSWER

ACTIVITY CORNER

FIND A WAY

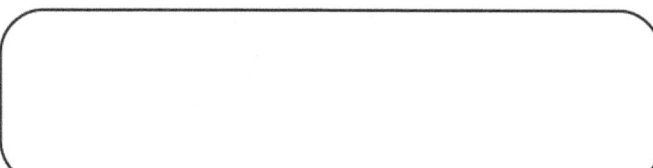

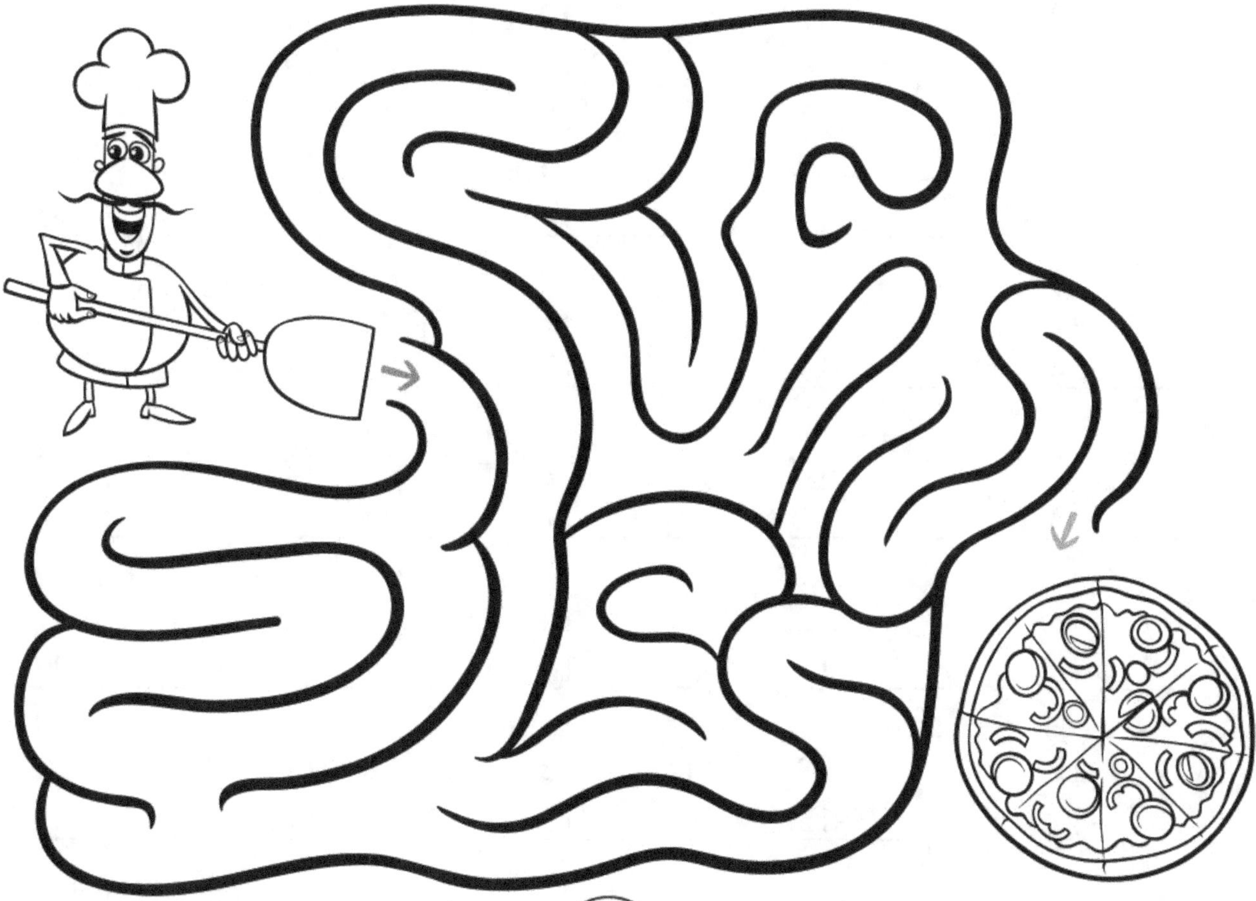

prepaze

SUBTRACTION 10 TO 15

Name: _____

Date: _____ Time: _____

Score: /50

1. 14 −13	2. 14 −11	3. 11 −11	4. 15 −13	5. 15 −14
6. 11 −11	7. 13 −11	8. 14 −12	9. 13 −11	10. 13 −13
11. 13 −12	12. 14 −12	13. 13 −13	14. 14 −12	15. 15 −13
16. 11 −11	17. 12 −12	18. 12 −12	19. 14 −13	20. 11 −11
21. 13 −11	22. 12 −11	23. 12 −11	24. 12 −12	25. 13 −12
26. 12 −12	27. 13 −11	28. 15 −14	29. 14 −13	30. 15 −15
31. 15 −14	32. 12 −12	33. 13 −12	34. 15 −11	35. 14 −11
36. 15 −13	37. 12 −11	38. 12 −11	39. 12 −11	40. 11 −11
41. 13 −13	42. 12 −11	43. 14 −12	44. 13 −11	45. 12 −11
46. 12 −11	47. 13 −13	48. 13 −13	49. 11 −11	50. 12 −11

prepaze

www.prepaze.com

SUBTRACTION 10 TO 15

Name: _____

Date: _____ Time: _____

Score: /50

1. 13
   -12
   ____

2. 11
   -11
   ____

3. 14
   -13
   ____

4. 14
   -13
   ____

5. 12
   -12
   ____

6. 13
   -12
   ____

7. 12
   -11
   ____

8. 11
   -11
   ____

9. 12
   -11
   ____

10. 14
   -14
   ____

11. 13
   -12
   ____

12. 12
   -12
   ____

13. 12
   -12
   ____

14. 15
   -13
   ____

15. 11
   -11
   ____

16. 14
   -13
   ____

17. 12
   -12
   ____

18. 12
   -12
   ____

19. 13
   -11
   ____

20. 12
   -12
   ____

21. 13
   -12
   ____

22. 15
   -14
   ____

23. 13
   -12
   ____

24. 14
   -14
   ____

25. 13
   -11
   ____

26. 12
   -12
   ____

27. 15
   -12
   ____

28. 12
   -12
   ____

29. 15
   -11
   ____

30. 12
   -11
   ____

31. 15
   -12
   ____

32. 14
   -13
   ____

33. 13
   -12
   ____

34. 12
   -11
   ____

35. 14
   -11
   ____

36. 15
   -14
   ____

37. 14
   -12
   ____

38. 14
   -12
   ____

39. 14
   -14
   ____

40. 12
   -12
   ____

41. 14
   -11
   ____

42. 14
   -13
   ____

43. 14
   -12
   ____

44. 11
   -11
   ____

45. 13
   -12
   ____

46. 12
   -11
   ____

47. 11
   -11
   ____

48. 11
   -11
   ____

49. 12
   -11
   ____

50. 12
   -12
   ____

prepaze

1. $14 - 13$	2. $13 - 13$	3. $13 - 12$	4. $12 - 12$	5. $15 - 12$
6. $13 - 11$	7. $13 - 13$	8. $14 - 14$	9. $14 - 13$	10. $13 - 12$
11. $14 - 13$	12. $13 - 11$	13. $12 - 11$	14. $11 - 11$	15. $12 - 12$
16. $15 - 14$	17. $13 - 13$	18. $11 - 11$	19. $12 - 12$	20. $15 - 15$
21. $14 - 11$	22. $11 - 11$	23. $13 - 13$	24. $11 - 11$	25. $14 - 11$
26. $13 - 13$	27. $12 - 11$	28. $12 - 11$	29. $12 - 11$	30. $14 - 13$
31. $13 - 11$	32. $13 - 11$	33. $13 - 12$	34. $11 - 11$	35. $12 - 11$
36. $14 - 12$	37. $13 - 12$	38. $12 - 11$	39. $13 - 13$	40. $13 - 12$
41. $12 - 12$	42. $15 - 11$	43. $12 - 11$	44. $12 - 12$	45. $14 - 13$
46. $14 - 11$	47. $13 - 13$	48. $12 - 12$	49. $12 - 11$	50. $15 - 11$

SUBTRACTION 10 TO 15

1. 13 −12	2. 14 −11	3. 13 −12	4. 12 −12	5. 12 −11
6. 13 −11	7. 11 −11	8. 11 −11	9. 13 −12	10. 14 −12
11. 14 −13	12. 13 −11	13. 13 −13	14. 12 −11	15. 14 −12
16. 12 −11	17. 11 −11	18. 13 −13	19. 13 −13	20. 13 −12
21. 14 −12	22. 11 −11	23. 12 −11	24. 15 −12	25. 13 −12
26. 12 −11	27. 14 −13	28. 14 −11	29. 15 −12	30. 13 −13
31. 14 −14	32. 15 −15	33. 12 −12	34. 15 −15	35. 14 −14
36. 14 −14	37. 14 −14	38. 11 −11	39. 12 −11	40. 12 −11
41. 14 −13	42. 12 −11	43. 13 −12	44. 12 −11	45. 15 −12
46. 12 −12	47. 12 −11	48. 15 −15	49. 13 −13	50. 13 −12

SUBTRACTION 10 TO 15

Name: _____
Date: _____ Time: _____
Score: /50

1.	14 -13	2.	13 -12	3.	14 -12	4.	13 -13	5.	15 -11
6.	14 -12	7.	15 -14	8.	11 -11	9.	12 -11	10.	14 -12
11.	12 -12	12.	12 -12	13.	14 -12	14.	13 -13	15.	12 -12
16.	13 -12	17.	12 -12	18.	14 -13	19.	12 -12	20.	15 -15
21.	14 -11	22.	12 -12	23.	11 -11	24.	13 -11	25.	13 -12
26.	15 -14	27.	12 -12	28.	14 -12	29.	11 -11	30.	12 -12
31.	12 -11	32.	12 -11	33.	12 -11	34.	11 -11	35.	14 -11
36.	15 -14	37.	15 -14	38.	11 -11	39.	14 -13	40.	11 -11
41.	13 -12	42.	13 -11	43.	12 -12	44.	15 -12	45.	13 -12
46.	14 -12	47.	12 -12	48.	12 -12	49.	11 -11	50.	11 -11

SUBTRACTION 10 TO 15

1. 14
   -12

2. 13
   -13

3. 14
   -11

4. 14
   -13

5. 14
   -13

6. 15
   -12

7. 15
   -11

8. 14
   -13

9. 13
   -12

10. 14
    -12

11. 15
    -12

12. 13
    -12

13. 14
    -13

14. 14
    -11

15. 14
    -12

16. 12
    -12

17. 14
    -13

18. 14
    -12

19. 11
    -11

20. 12
    -12

21. 14
    -12

22. 12
    -12

23. 12
    -11

24. 12
    -11

25. 13
    -12

26. 14
    -13

27. 13
    -13

28. 12
    -12

29. 15
    -11

30. 12
    -11

31. 12
    -12

32. 12
    -11

33. 13
    -12

34. 14
    -13

35. 12
    -11

36. 13
    -11

37. 13
    -12

38. 13
    -12

39. 14
    -13

40. 13
    -12

41. 12
    -11

42. 12
    -11

43. 12
    -11

44. 11
    -11

45. 14
    -14

46. 14
    -13

47. 12
    -11

48. 12
    -11

49. 15
    -12

50. 15
    -13

SUBTRACTION 10 TO 15

1. 11 -11	2. 13 -11	3. 12 -11	4. 12 -12	5. 15 -12
6. 12 -11	7. 14 -13	8. 13 -11	9. 14 -12	10. 12 -12
11. 15 -12	12. 14 -14	13. 13 -13	14. 12 -11	15. 12 -11
16. 12 -11	17. 12 -12	18. 12 -12	19. 13 -12	20. 13 -12
21. 14 -12	22. 14 -12	23. 13 -11	24. 13 -11	25. 14 -14
26. 14 -13	27. 12 -11	28. 12 -11	29. 15 -13	30. 13 -13
31. 14 -11	32. 13 -12	33. 13 -12	34. 15 -14	35. 12 -11
36. 13 -11	37. 13 -12	38. 12 -12	39. 15 -14	40. 13 -12
41. 11 -11	42. 12 -12	43. 14 -13	44. 12 -11	45. 14 -11
46. 13 -12	47. 14 -12	48. 13 -12	49. 14 -13	50. 12 -11

SUBTRACTION 10 TO 15

1.
```
   13
 -12
_____
```

2.
```
   14
 -12
_____
```

3.
```
   14
 -13
_____
```

4.
```
   12
 -11
_____
```

5.
```
   14
 -13
_____
```

6.
```
   15
 -15
_____
```

7.
```
   12
 -12
_____
```

8.
```
   13
 -11
_____
```

9.
```
   13
 -12
_____
```

10.
```
   14
 -11
_____
```

11.
```
   14
 -12
_____
```

12.
```
   14
 -13
_____
```

13.
```
   13
 -13
_____
```

14.
```
   14
 -11
_____
```

15.
```
   12
 -12
_____
```

16.
```
   15
 -14
_____
```

17.
```
   13
 -12
_____
```

18.
```
   14
 -12
_____
```

19.
```
   13
 -13
_____
```

20.
```
   13
 -13
_____
```

21.
```
   13
 -13
_____
```

22.
```
   13
 -12
_____
```

23.
```
   11
 -11
_____
```

24.
```
   11
 -11
_____
```

25.
```
   14
 -13
_____
```

26.
```
   12
 -11
_____
```

27.
```
   13
 -12
_____
```

28.
```
   11
 -11
_____
```

29.
```
   13
 -12
_____
```

30.
```
   14
 -12
_____
```

31.
```
   12
 -11
_____
```

32.
```
   15
 -14
_____
```

33.
```
   12
 -11
_____
```

34.
```
   15
 -14
_____
```

35.
```
   14
 -14
_____
```

36.
```
   12
 -11
_____
```

37.
```
   13
 -13
_____
```

38.
```
   14
 -14
_____
```

39.
```
   14
 -12
_____
```

40.
```
   12
 -12
_____
```

41.
```
   14
 -12
_____
```

42.
```
   14
 -14
_____
```

43.
```
   12
 -11
_____
```

44.
```
   14
 -13
_____
```

45.
```
   12
 -11
_____
```

46.
```
   14
 -12
_____
```

47.
```
   12
 -12
_____
```

48.
```
   11
 -11
_____
```

49.
```
   14
 -11
_____
```

50.
```
   11
 -11
_____
```

WORD PROBLEMS
SUBTRACTION 10 TO 15

1. Captain catches 15 fish. He puts 12 back. How many does he have left?

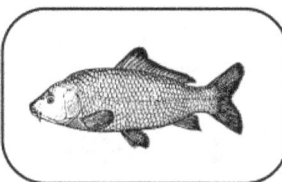

 **ANSWER**

2. Joan has 13 books. He completed reading 10 books. How many books he is left out to read?

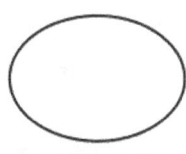 **ANSWER**

3. 11 wreaths were in the basket. Some of the wreaths were removed from the basket. Now there are 2 wreaths. How many wreaths were removed from the basket?

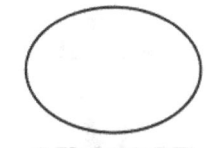 **ANSWER**

4. John's birthday cake had 13 candles. He blew up only 4 candles. How many candles are still there to blow?

 **ANSWER**

Name: _____

Date: _____ Time: _____

5. Jade had some strawberries. She gave 6 of them to Helen. Now Jade has 14 strawberries. How many strawberries did Jade have at first?

ANSWER

6. Jack had 16 candies. He gave some of them to Nico. Now Jack has 11 candies. How many candies did Jack give Nico?

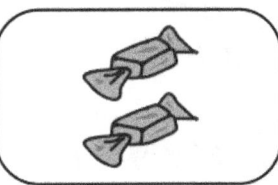

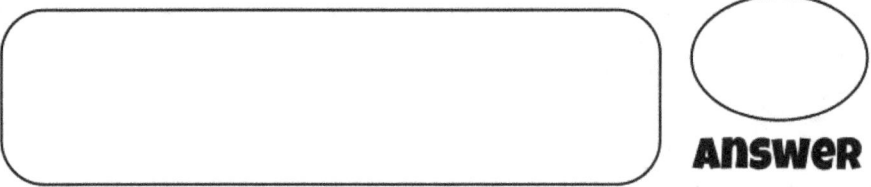

ANSWER

7. May had 15 ice creams. She gave 7 of them to Ella. How many does May have left?

ANSWER

8. Jack had 15 cupcakes. He gave 8 of them to Luna. How many cupcakes did Jack have left?

ANSWER

WORD PROBLEMS
SUBTRACTION 10 TO 15

9. Jim had 15 feathers. He gave some of them to Jill. Now Jim has 4 feathers. How many feathers did Jim give Jill?

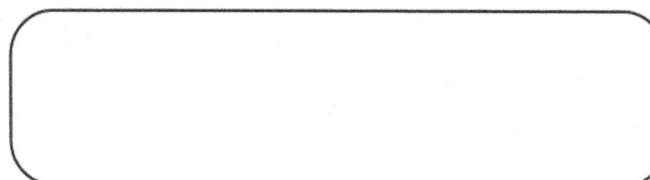

ANSWER

10. Dawn had 12 candies. She gave 7 of them to Ian. How many candies does Dawn have left?

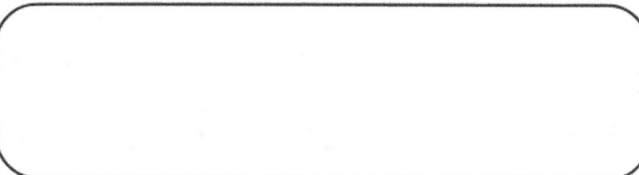

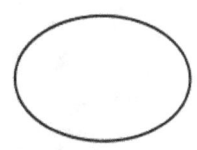

ANSWER

11. There were 14 bees in the garden. 8 of them flew away. How many bees were in the garden?

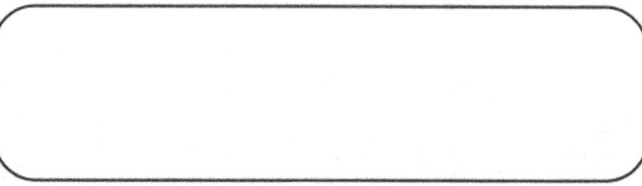

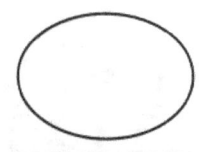

ANSWER

12. Lynn had 13 crayons. She gave some of them to Mike. Now Lynn has 7 crayons. How many crayons did Lynn give Mike?

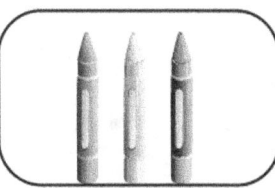

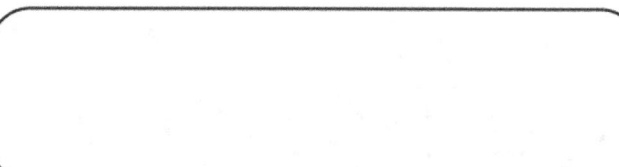

ANSWER

SUBTRACT THE NUMBERS

13 – 7 =

15 – 10 =

9 – 3 =

12 – 7 =

WORD PROBLEMS
SUBTRACTION 10 TO 15

Name: _____
Date: _____ Time: _____

13. Kat had 11 action figures. She gave 6 of them to Cara. How many action figures does Kat have left?

ANSWER

14. Mia had 15 blocks. She gave some of them to Miles. Now Mia has 14 blocks. How many blocks did Mia give Miles?

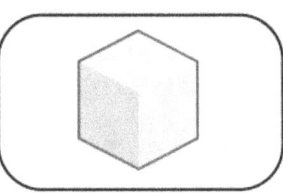 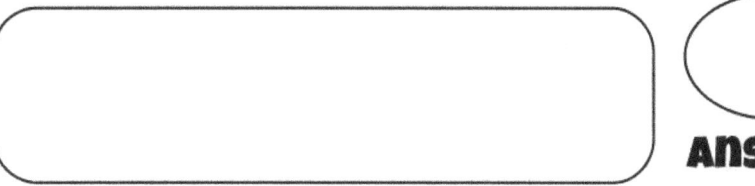

ANSWER

15. David 11 apples. He gave 8 of them to Blaire. How many apples does David have?

 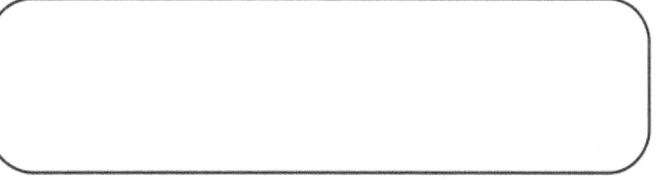

ANSWER

16. John 15 jelly beans. He gave 6 of them to Brooke. How many jelly beans does John?

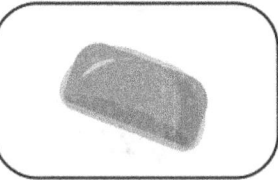 

ANSWER

Name: _____

Date: _____ Time: _____

17. Rosie 12 ribbons. She gave 6 of them to Tess. How many ribbons does Rosie have?

answer

18. There are 11 sparrows in the tree. 5 of them flew away. How many sparrows are in the tree?

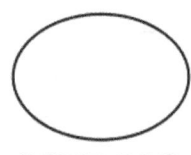

answer

19. Mike 14 doughnuts. He gave 6 of them to May. How many doughnuts does Mike have?

answer

20. There were 15 caterpillars in the garden. 5 of them crawled away. How many caterpillars are in the garden now?

answer

WORD PROBLEMS
SUBTRACTION 10 TO 15

Name: _____
Date: _____ Time: _____

21. Tom 11 balloons. He gave 8 of them to Penny. How many balloons does Tom have now?

ANSWER

22. Mike had 13 gifts. He gave 11 of them to Dawn. How many gifts does Mike have now?

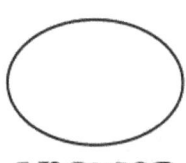

ANSWER

23. John 11 treats. He gave 11 of them to Julia. How many treats does John have now?

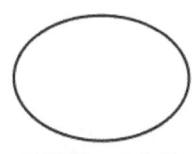

ANSWER

24. There were 14 sharks near the shore. 14 of them swam away. How many sharks ware near the shore?

ANSWER

prepaze

25. Larry's birthday cake had 11 candles. He blew only 7 candles. How many candles are still there to blow?

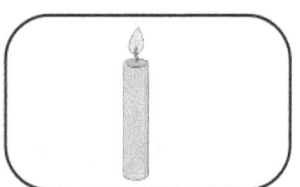

ANSWER

CONNECT THE DOTS

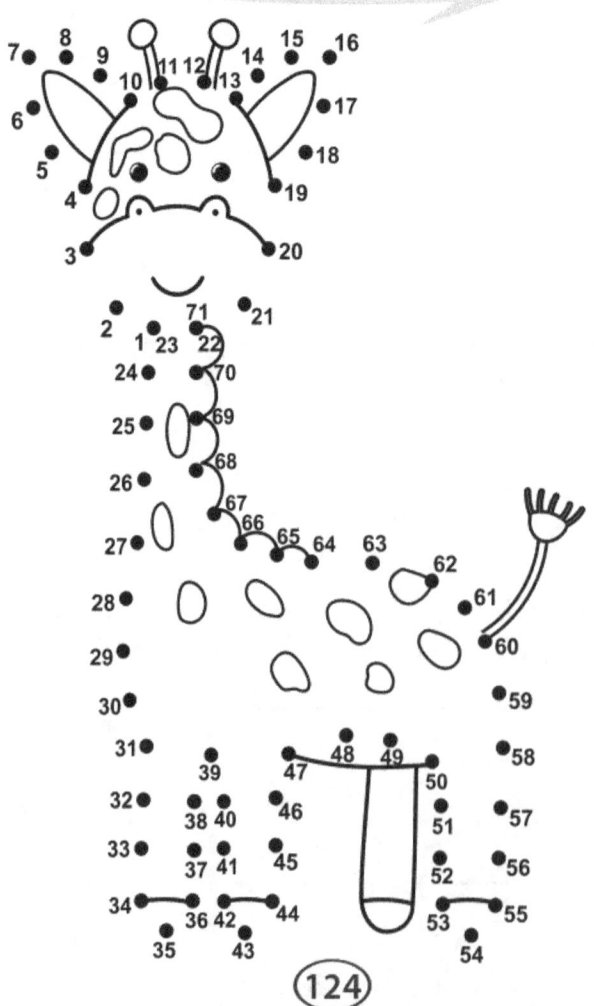

SUBTRACTION 0 TO 15

Name: _____

Date: _____ Time: _____

Score: /50

1. 4 −0	2. 8 −1	3. 1 −1	4. 4 −1	5. 13 −7
6. 13 −9	7. 0 −0	8. 7 −3	9. 5 −4	10. 1 −1
11. 0 −0	12. 0 −0	13. 10 −9	14. 8 −0	15. 4 −1
16. 1 −1	17. 13 −2	18. 14 −4	19. 6 −5	20. 6 −6
21. 3 −2	22. 1 −0	23. 3 −1	24. 1 −0	25. 12 −0
26. 15 −15	27. 7 −0	28. 2 −2	29. 2 −0	30. 14 −13
31. 13 −8	32. 3 −1	33. 2 −1	34. 8 −6	35. 6 −2
36. 9 −5	37. 7 −5	38. 12 −5	39. 8 −7	40. 3 −2
41. 14 −3	42. 5 −2	43. 12 −2	44. 4 −3	45. 8 −8
46. 9 −7	47. 6 −2	48. 8 −7	49. 9 −9	50. 4 −1

prepaze

SUBTRACTION 0 TO 15

Name: _____

Date: _____ Time: _____

Score: /50

1.	2.	3.	4.	5.
13 -11	8 -1	9 -3	10 -8	10 -7

6.	7.	8.	9.	10.
4 -3	1 -1	12 -10	6 -5	14 -11

11.	12.	13.	14.	15.
8 -7	12 -6	9 -5	4 -4	12 -10

16.	17.	18.	19.	20.
13 -7	7 -7	3 -1	11 -9	6 -2

21.	22.	23.	24.	25.
8 -5	1 -1	1 -1	0 -0	1 -1

26.	27.	28.	29.	30.
13 -3	3 -0	9 -1	10 -8	8 -8

31.	32.	33.	34.	35.
11 -3	2 -0	1 -1	2 -1	2 -0

36.	37.	38.	39.	40.
2 -0	8 -5	3 -0	7 -5	12 -2

41.	42.	43.	44.	45.
7 -4	7 -2	13 -13	2 -2	6 -3

46.	47.	48.	49.	50.
0 -0	7 -2	10 -9	14 -6	14 -13

SUBTRACTION 0 TO 15

1. $10 - 1$	2. $9 - 9$	3. $12 - 8$	4. $5 - 5$	5. $6 - 3$
6. $12 - 10$	7. $10 - 1$	8. $11 - 1$	9. $14 - 13$	10. $2 - 0$
11. $8 - 7$	12. $0 - 0$	13. $4 - 1$	14. $6 - 1$	15. $3 - 1$
16. $2 - 1$	17. $12 - 5$	18. $3 - 3$	19. $3 - 3$	20. $1 - 0$
21. $4 - 2$	22. $9 - 6$	23. $6 - 5$	24. $12 - 11$	25. $11 - 2$
26. $3 - 2$	27. $14 - 0$	28. $10 - 9$	29. $1 - 1$	30. $10 - 9$
31. $2 - 1$	32. $8 - 0$	33. $13 - 2$	34. $14 - 3$	35. $5 - 2$
36. $5 - 4$	37. $15 - 3$	38. $14 - 13$	39. $0 - 0$	40. $0 - 0$
41. $8 - 7$	42. $11 - 6$	43. $12 - 5$	44. $3 - 3$	45. $10 - 8$
46. $14 - 2$	47. $10 - 3$	48. $8 - 1$	49. $12 - 2$	50. $0 - 0$

1. 11
    -7
    _____

2. 13
    -5
    _____

3. 13
    -0
    _____

4. 3
    -1
    _____

5. 5
    -1
    _____

6. 12
    -5
    _____

7. 10
    -4
    _____

8. 12
    -7
    _____

9. 11
    -9
    _____

10. 15
    -14
    _____

11. 5
    -1
    _____

12. 7
    -4
    _____

13. 9
    -2
    _____

14. 14
    -12
    _____

15. 3
    -2
    _____

16. 14
    -9
    _____

17. 11
    -3
    _____

18. 6
    -5
    _____

19. 13
    -10
    _____

20. 14
    -4
    _____

21. 12
    -4
    _____

22. 8
    -3
    _____

23. 2
    -2
    _____

24. 12
    -7
    _____

25. 12
    -2
    _____

26. 14
    -4
    _____

27. 7
    -6
    _____

28. 12
    -5
    _____

29. 9
    -3
    _____

30. 2
    -1
    _____

31. 2
    -1
    _____

32. 7
    -3
    _____

33. 2
    -1
    _____

34. 13
    -0
    _____

35. 6
    -5
    _____

36. 13
    -12
    _____

37. 0
    -0
    _____

38. 8
    -4
    _____

39. 4
    -2
    _____

40. 2
    -0
    _____

41. 4
    -4
    _____

42. 5
    -3
    _____

43. 15
    -13
    _____

44. 9
    -5
    _____

45. 12
    -2
    _____

46. 3
    -1
    _____

47. 14
    -14
    _____

48. 8
    -4
    _____

49. 11
    -4
    _____

50. 1
    -0
    _____

1.	3 -3	2.	2 -1	3.	2 -0	4.	5 -3	5.	13 -9
6.	5 -3	7.	4 -0	8.	5 -3	9.	6 -4	10.	13 -13
11.	7 -3	12.	6 -5	13.	1 -1	14.	12 -12	15.	6 -5
16.	15 -9	17.	13 -12	18.	14 -2	19.	8 -4	20.	7 -4
21.	14 -7	22.	10 -10	23.	12 -10	24.	1 -0	25.	14 -13
26.	7 -2	27.	12 -6	28.	5 -4	29.	12 -3	30.	0 -0
31.	15 -10	32.	12 -11	33.	10 -5	34.	15 -4	35.	8 -2
36.	12 -5	37.	11 -5	38.	7 -1	39.	11 -2	40.	1 -1
41.	6 -2	42.	15 -1	43.	0 -0	44.	0 -0	45.	15 -1
46.	5 -1	47.	4 -4	48.	7 -1	49.	10 -8	50.	2 -1

SUBTRACTION 0 TO 15

1.	1 −1	2.	15 −14	3.	5 −1	4.	10 −2	5.	6 −4
6.	12 −12	7.	14 −2	8.	13 −4	9.	8 −7	10.	5 −2
11.	14 −9	12.	7 −1	13.	2 −2	14.	8 −6	15.	13 −8
16.	7 −1	17.	15 −5	18.	14 −8	19.	14 −11	20.	9 −2
21.	15 −11	22.	5 −2	23.	7 −4	24.	1 −0	25.	5 −4
26.	14 −4	27.	14 −10	28.	1 −0	29.	8 −6	30.	14 −12
31.	9 −2	32.	11 −7	33.	7 −3	34.	8 −7	35.	11 −4
36.	12 −7	37.	14 −4	38.	14 −11	39.	13 −1	40.	6 −5
41.	13 −5	42.	14 −13	43.	11 −4	44.	8 −5	45.	8 −6
46.	2 −2	47.	1 −1	48.	9 −2	49.	11 −9	50.	12 −11

SUBTRACTION 0 TO 15

Name: _____

Date: _____ Time: _____

Score: /50

1. 14 -1	2. 6 -4	3. 7 -5	4. 15 -11	5. 5 -1
6. 3 -3	7. 2 -2	8. 6 -3	9. 11 -9	10. 5 -2
11. 1 -1	12. 7 -4	13. 1 -1	14. 2 -2	15. 5 -4
16. 1 -1	17. 1 -0	18. 8 -6	19. 13 -4	20. 0 -0
21. 7 -7	22. 10 -3	23. 12 -9	24. 0 -0	25. 12 -0
26. 3 -1	27. 3 -0	28. 10 -8	29. 7 -5	30. 11 -5
31. 4 -4	32. 11 -1	33. 14 -13	34. 9 -6	35. 8 -2
36. 3 -3	37. 4 -2	38. 5 -5	39. 1 -0	40. 14 -0
41. 9 -0	42. 9 -0	43. 11 -1	44. 4 -1	45. 12 -5
46. 4 -4	47. 9 -4	48. 14 -3	49. 12 -4	50. 7 -4

prepaze

SUBTRACTION
0 TO 15

Name: _____

Date: _____ Time: _____

Score:
/50

1. 5 -5	2. 2 -1	3. 12 -9	4. 13 -7	5. 8 -3
6. 11 -3	7. 13 -11	8. 4 -2	9. 1 -1	10. 12 -4
11. 3 -1	12. 14 -4	13. 14 -13	14. 7 -5	15. 4 -3
16. 13 -5	17. 13 -12	18. 12 -5	19. 10 -6	20. 5 -2
21. 7 -2	22. 2 -1	23. 9 -6	24. 9 -4	25. 3 -3
26. 4 -2	27. 3 -0	28. 12 -3	29. 8 -8	30. 11 -8
31. 1 -0	32. 1 -1	33. 9 -5	34. 8 -6	35. 12 -8
36. 1 -1	37. 13 -6	38. 6 -0	39. 9 -8	40. 9 -6
41. 10 -4	42. 7 -6	43. 7 -3	44. 2 -1	45. 10 -10
46. 7 -3	47. 11 -8	48. 9 -1	49. 7 -2	50. 11 -0

FIND THE 10 DIFFERENCES

prepaze

WORD PROBLEMS
SUBTRACTION 0 TO 15

Name: _____
Date: _____ Time: _____

1. There are 7 marbles in a box. Dorothy removes 4 marbles. How many marbles are still in the box?

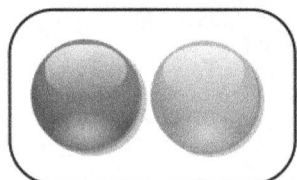 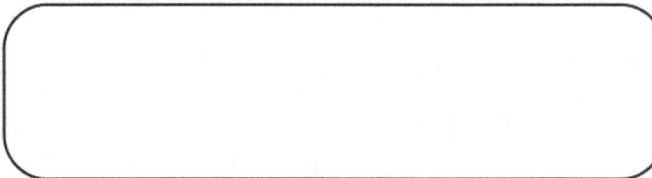 

ANSWER

2. Jane weighs 16 pounds. Joshua weighs 2 pounds. How much heavier is Jane than Joshua?

ANSWER

3. There are 15 erasers in a box. Ralph takes 7 erasers. How many are left?

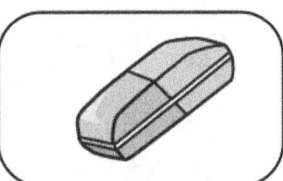 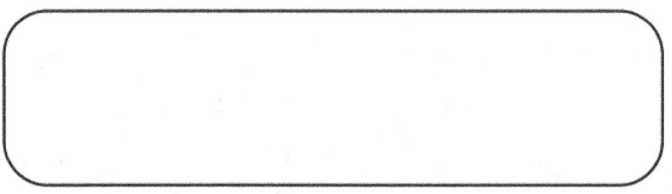 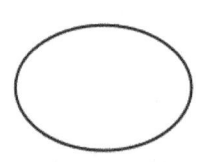

ANSWER

4. Jerry has 12 eggs. Edward has 5 eggs. How many more eggs does Jerry have than Edward?

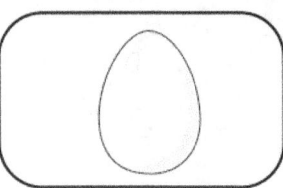  

ANSWER

WORD PROBLEMS
SUBTRACTION 0 TO 15

5. Emily has 15 peanuts. She gives 8 peanuts to Tim. How many peanuts will Emily have left?

ANSWER

6. If there are 15 apples in a box and Jade takes out 9 apples How many apples will be left in the box?

ANSWER

7. There are 13 chairs in the hallway. The helpers remove 2 chairs. How many chairs are left in the hallway now?

ANSWER

8. There are 5 farmers working in a field. 3 of them leave for lunch break. How many are still working in the field?

ANSWER

prepaze

WORD PROBLEMS
SUBTRACTION 0 TO 15

Name: _____
Date: _____ Time: _____

9. Adam has 7 fishes in his tank. He gave 3 to Eve. How many fish are left in his tank?

ANSWER

10. Ann went for a walk with his father. He bought 8 balloons from the balloon seller. 2 balloons flew away. How many balloons left?

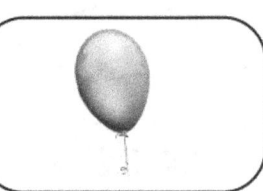

ANSWER

11. Lora's father bought 9 packs of chocolates. He gave 2 packs to Lora. How many packs are left?

ANSWER

12. Sam bought 7 oranges. He gave 2 oranges to his friend. He wanted to give the remaining oranges to his mother. How many oranges did he give to his mother?

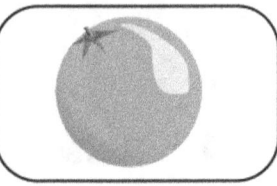

ANSWER

COLORING ACTIVITY

Name: _____

Date: _____ Time: _____

13. Michelle has 10 crayons. He gave 6 crayons to Bella. How many crayons does Michelle have?

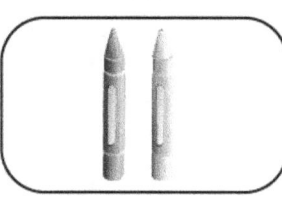

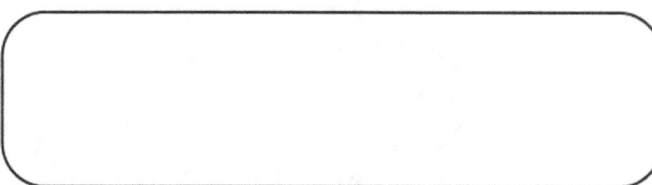

ANSWER

14. There were 4 rats running in Eve's house. The cats ate 2 rats. How many rats were left?

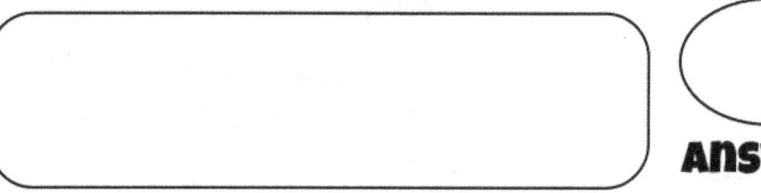

ANSWER

15. Andrew bought 15 gifts to distribute to his friends. He distributed 9 gifts. How many gifts does he have left?

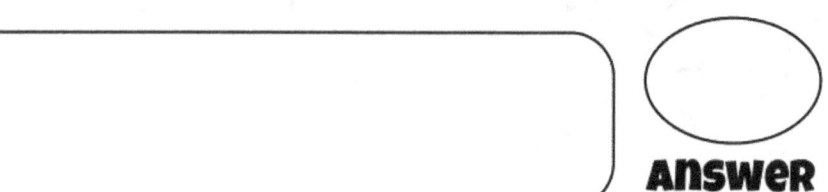

ANSWER

16. Joey had 12 giraffe toys. He lost 3 of them. How many giraffe toys does Joey have now?

ANSWER

WORD PROBLEMS
SUBTRACTION 0 TO 15

17. Daniel removes 2 blocks from a box. There were originally 8 blocks in the jar. How many blocks are left in the box?

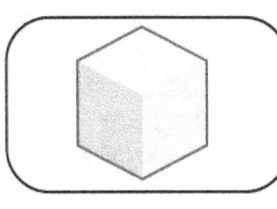

ANSWER

18. Billy has 5 stickers. He gives 4 to Harry. How many stickers will Billy have left?

ANSWER

19. Jason starts with 9 crayons. He gives 4 crayons to Joshua.. How many crayons does Jason have now?

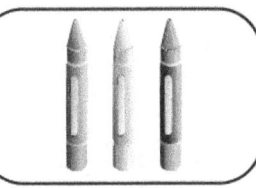

ANSWER

20. Randy has 6 stickers. He loses 1. How many stickers does Randy have with him?

ANSWER

prepaze

WORD PROBLEMS
SUBTRACTION 0 TO 15

21. Lawrence has 8 bowling pins. He loses 6. How many bowling pins does Lawrence have left?

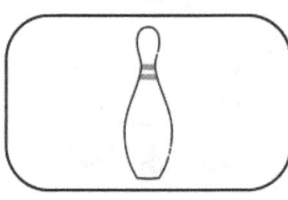  

ANSWER

22. Doris weighs 14 pounds. Janet weighs 13 pounds. How much heavier is Doris than Janet?

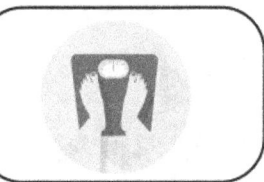 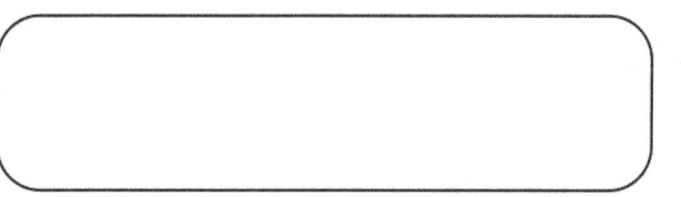

ANSWER

23. If there are 7 marbles in a box and Gregory removes 7 marbles, how many marbles are left in the box?

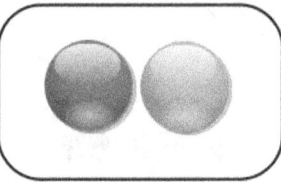 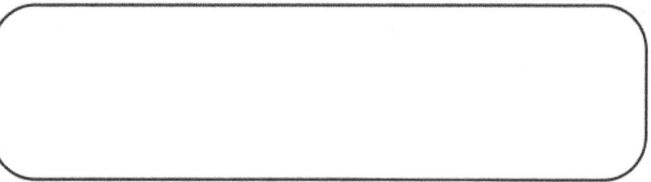 

ANSWER

24. If there are 9 cards in a box and Carol takes out 3 cards, how many cards are still there in the box?

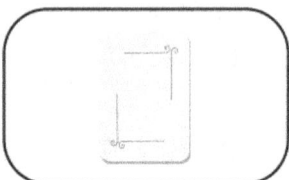  

ANSWER

WORD PROBLEMS
SUBTRACTION 0 TO 15

Name: ____________________

Date: __________ Time: __________

25. Ralph starts with 11 bowling pins. He bowls 6. How many bowling pins does Ralph have standing?

ANSWER

ACTIVITY CORNER

FIND A WAY

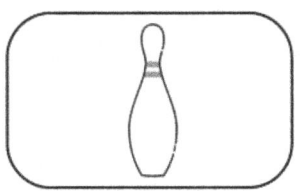

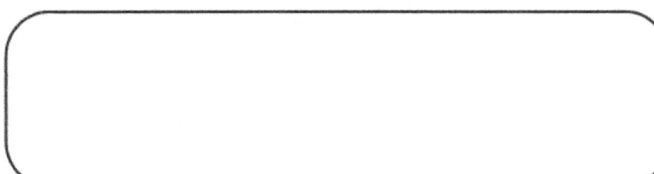

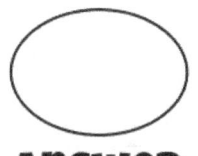

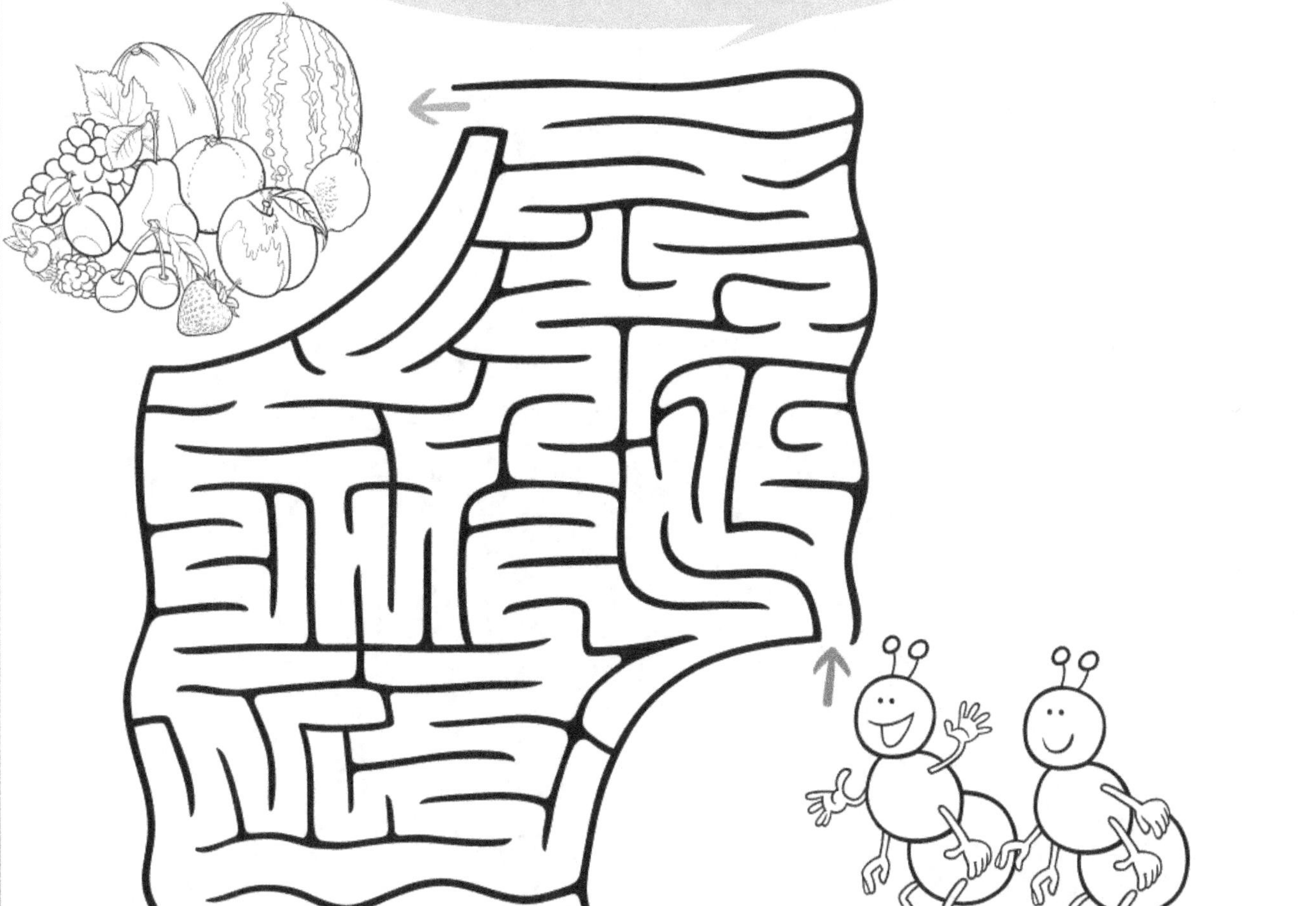

ANSWERS FOR WORD PROBLEMS

ADDITION 0 TO 5

1. 3
2. 4
3. 2
4. 3
5. 2
6. 3
7. 4
8. 5
9. 4
10. 5
11. 5
12. 4
13. 2
14. 3
15. 5
16. 4
17. 2
18. 3
19. 4
20. 5
21. 5
22. 2
23. 4
24. 3
25. 5

ADDITION 6 TO 10

1. 7
2. 10
3. 8
4. 9
5. 7
6. 6
7. 8
8. 10
9. 9
10. 7
11. 6
12. 8
13. 10
14. 8
15. 6
16. 7
17. 10
18. 9
19. 9
20. 7
21. 6
22. 8
23. 9
24. 10
25. 9

ANSWERS FOR WORD PROBLEMS

ADDITION 11 TO 15

1. 11
2. 13
3. 15
4. 14
5. 12
6. 14
7. 11
8. 15
9. 13
10. 12
11. 14
12. 11
13. 15
14. 13
15. 15
16. 14
17. 12
18. 13
19. 14
20. 15
21. 11
22. 12
23. 14
24. 13
25. 15

ADDITION 0 TO 15

1. 2
2. 3
3. 5
4. 4
5. 2
6. 4
7. 5
8. 3
9. 6
10. 8
11. 7
12. 10
13. 9
14. 8
15. 6
16. 7
17. 11
18. 12
19. 14
20. 13
21. 15
22. 12
23. 13
24. 14
25. 15

ANSWERS FOR WORD PROBLEMS

SUBTRACTION 0 TO 5

1.	3
2.	1
3.	1
4.	2
5.	0
6.	1
7.	2
8.	2
9.	0
10.	1
11.	3
12.	3
13.	1
14.	3
15.	0
16.	3
17.	2
18.	2
19.	2
20.	2
21.	1
22.	1
23.	4
24.	1
25.	4

SUBTRACTION 6 TO 10

1.	4
2.	2
3.	1
4.	4
5.	1
6.	0
7.	4
8.	3
9.	2
10.	7
11.	2
12.	2
13.	1
14.	2
15.	1
16.	1
17.	3
18.	2
19.	2
20.	4
21.	1
22.	2
23.	3
24.	Yes
25.	4

ANSWERS FOR WORD PROBLEMS

SUBTRACTION 11 TO 15

1. 3
2. 3
3. 9
4. 9
5. 8
6. 5
7. 8
8. 7
9. 11
10. 5
11. 6
12. 6
13. 5
14. 1
15. 3
16. 9
17. 6
18. 6
19. 8
20. 10
21. 3
22. 2
23. 0
24. 0
25. 4

SUBTRACTION 0 TO 15

1. 3
2. 14
3. 8
4. 7
5. 7
6. 6
7. 1
8. 2
9. 4
10. 6
11. 7
12. 5
13. 4
14. 2
15. 6
16. 9
17. 6
18. 1
19. 5
20. 5
21. 2
22. 1
23. 0
24. 6
25. 5

prepaze

LET'S PLAY A GAME

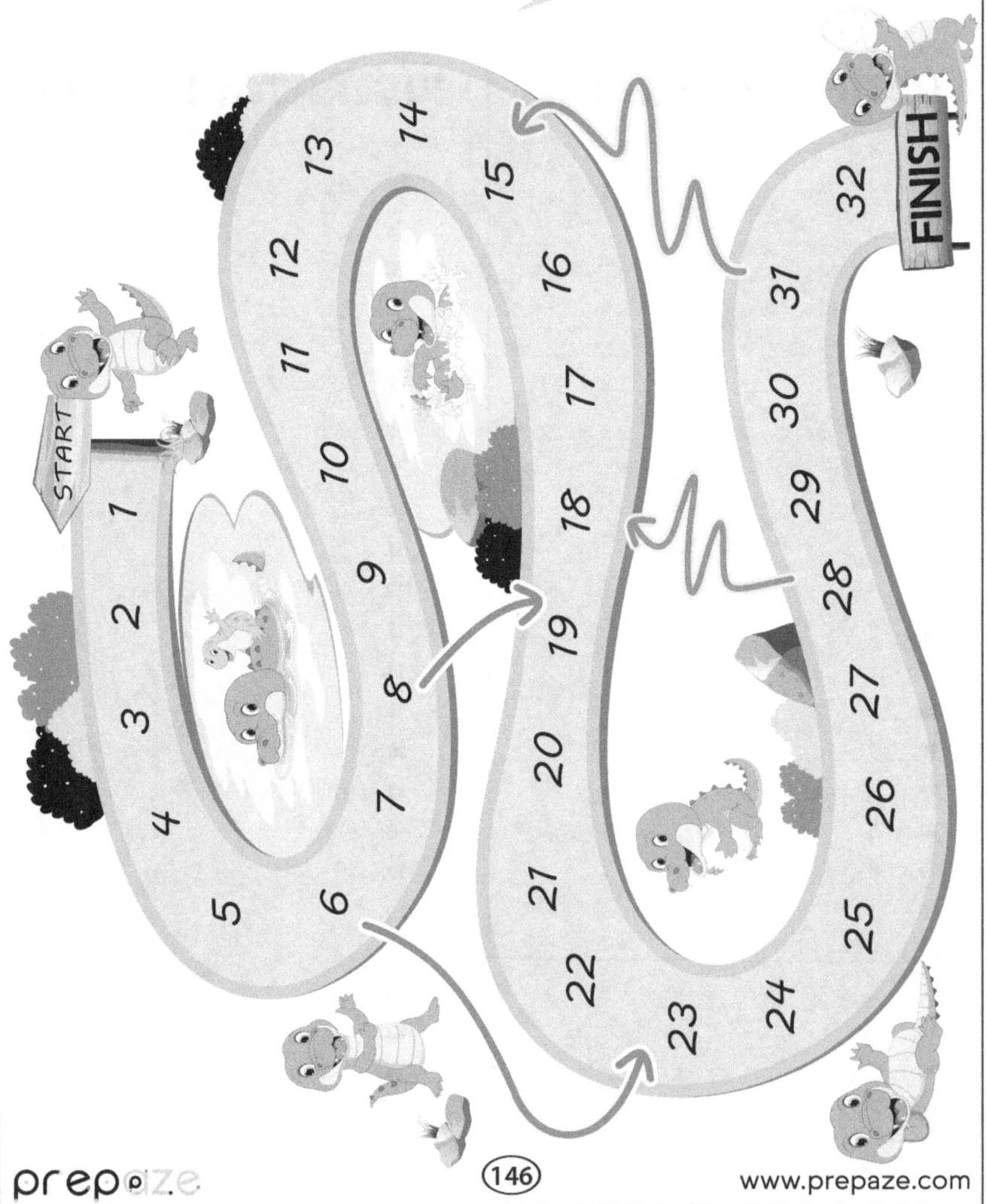

START

1 2 3 4 5 6 7 8 9 10 11 12 13 14 15 16 17 18 19 20 21 22 23 24 25 26 27 28 29 30 31 32

FINISH

www.ingramcontent.com/pod-product-compliance
Lightning Source LLC
Chambersburg PA
CBHW080958120626
46546CB00010B/2951